THE RURAL MUSE

THE RURAL MUSE

Studies in the
Peasant Poetry of England

Rayner Unwin

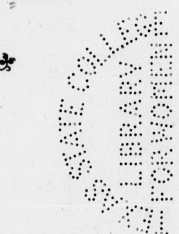

George Allen and Unwin Ltd.
Ruskin House Museum Street London

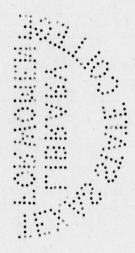

*Printed in Great Britain
in 11 point Bembo type
by Unwin Brothers Limited
Woking and London*

Contents

To Professor H. E. Rollins and Professor D. Bush, who gave me boldness to undertake these studies, I owe respect and gratitude. I also gladly acknowledge my indebtedness to Mr. Alvin Whitley, Mr. Malcolm Barnes and Mr. David Unwin for the help and encouragement they have so willingly given me. The finished book I dedicate to my wife, who had the patience to endure its composition.

Preface

The subject of this book is the studied attempts in verse of the English landworker; only indirectly is it concerned with the ballads, catches and songs circulated orally and by broadsheet up to this day.

Compared with the vigorous poetic output of the peasantry of Scotland and Wales the English peasant-poet sings in a distinctly minor key: the music is faintly heard and for long periods the words have been lost. There has been no consecutive tradition, little public recognition or encouragement, and no sturdy spirit to walk

> in glory and in joy
> Following his plough, along the mountain-side.

Yet the peasants and labourers of England have not, throughout the centuries, been a clod-bound, inexpressive race. Their occupation has been recognized since the earliest days as one dearly loved by the Muses, and poverty and hardship has never staunched the flow of poetry from inspired pens.

The pursuit of poetry is seldom easy. In the case of the majority of the writers mentioned in these pages it was intolerably hard. They struggled against insufficient education, lack of leisure, and of the necessities of life, to achieve transitory, and in a few cases a deserved and lasting, fame. Few of these writers have been memorialized, and the meandering stream of poetry that sprang from the land itself has never before been mapped. For many years its course was indistinguishable amongst the general flow of vernacular writing. Not until the early eighteenth century did the poetry of the uneducated landsman become detached from the strong, turbulent currents of more sophisticated verse. Throughout that century, when poetic expression was a well-disseminated but stylized medium of expression, the factual, realistic voice of the peasant-poet could occasionally be heard amongst the obstinate lovers of the town. With the coming of the industrial revolution and the completion of the process of enclosure that, over the centuries, brought prosperity to the country but extinction to the

9

peasant class, such poets were eclipsed, and the artisans largely took their place as makers of occupational verse.

The names that spring most readily to mind when peasant-poets are mentioned—Burns, Hogg and the host of makers and bards from Scotland and Wales—are the very ones that are excluded, for they would inevitably outweigh the more frail English contingent. There are no principal actors, no plot and no dénouement; but there are plenty of small parts, and in the wings some famous, and many forgotten, players push themselves forward as candidates for the stage. With such a cast in reserve there is a danger of overcrowding. It is almost relevant to touch on such a bewildering proportion of English poetry that the first function of a critic must be to define his subject and his terms of reference.

The scope of this study is limited to the peasant-poet, and indeed, if it ventured far into the realm of poets who had struggled from impoverished and lowly circumstances to express themselves in verse, many volumes would be needed and the chronicle would embrace half the history of English letters. Besides, an anthology of success or hard-luck stories would make sorry reading. Nevertheless it is often difficult to define a peasant-poet, and satisfy one's definition by reference to biography. Bloomfield was a shoemaker when he wrote *The Farmer's Boy*, and Williams, though he lived in the country, worked in the railway factory at Swindon. The net must be cast wide, at the risk of including figures who stand at the fringe of understanding, in order to include those men, who by reason of their heightened susceptibility to impressions, could appreciate without experiencing "the rustic wonder of the village-boy"; poets as Keats imagined them, who could negate their identity, and be "continually in for—and filling some other Body." This does not include Wordsworth, who saw with his own eyes, but could not surrender his personality to peck with the sparrow in the gravel. It only includes Thomson inasmuch as his influence profoundly affected all future generations of peasant-poets. But it does include the poetry of Barnes, and some of the works of Relph and Crabbe.

The final judgment on who shall qualify as a peasant-poet must rest with the individual reader. Duck, Bloomfield, Clare, and Williams are obviously eligible, but the gallery of eighteenth-century poetasters who fill the fourth chapter are random portraits: there are many others that could equally well be substituted. The purpose of the chapter is to represent untrained poetic endeavour at that time, and lowly birth has such a proud and long heritage of achievement that to be selective must inevitably be invidious.

Sometimes I have strayed from the peasant to the mechanic muse, and although in doing so I have exceeded my brief, the comparison is not uninteresting. Townsmen as well as countrymen in their desire for expression in verse reflect the shifting moods of an enlarging, poetry-conscious public. In terms of quantity there was a definite relationship between the practitioners of verse and the public interest that might support them. The eighteenth-century reader still accepted poetry as easily as prose, and with the spread of literacy an increasing section of the population read and wrote verses. "It is a difficult matter to account why," wrote Richard West to his friend Walpole in 1737, "but certain it is that all people, from the duke's coronet to the thresher's flail are desirous to be poets."

To devote space to Thomson and Crabbe deserves a further word of explanation. Thomson was a well-educated Scot, and certainly not a peasant. He would have no place in this study were it not for the profound effect that *The Seasons* had upon succeeding generations of country poets. His poem is a touchstone against which almost every other poet in this book tested his own works, or had them judged. Few books could have been read by a larger public or been so reverently received. Nearly a century after its publication Coleridge, who picked up a worn-out copy of *The Seasons* in the inn at Linstock, exclaimed to Hazlitt, "*That* is true fame."

Crabbe might with more justification be called a peasant-poet. He was certainly poorly-born and ill-educated. He had himself experienced poverty and hardship. But it is not for these reasons that he has a place in these pages, nor on account of his followers or imitators. Crabbe saw with clearer vision, and wrote with less dissimulation, than any labourer or artisan about "what form the real picture of the poor." After one has read the effusions of many uneducated poets real life and written life seem to become two altogether separate considerations.

Crabbe's early poems are salutary to read because they do not extenuate the realities that every peasant-poet to some extent experienced in life, but glossed over in his art.

It would be pleasant to close this introduction with a summary of the peasant-poet movement. Southey (whose prefatory essay to the poems of John Jones was the first acknowledgment of the independent tradition of the uneducated poet) had felt justified in trying. Writing in 1831 he considered "that as the Age of Reason had commenced, and we were advancing with quick step in the March of Intellect, Mr. Jones would in all likelihood be the last versifier of his class." Southey was wrong in regarding the movement as finished. With the exception of Taylor the uneducated poets that he memorialized were drawn entirely from the eighteenth century; neither Burns nor Bloomfield had achieved their historical perspective, Clare, if not unknown, was overlooked, and half a century was to pass before the birth of Williams. To bring the history of the peasant-poet to a close would obviously be as rash to attempt now as it has proved to be in Southey's time. Alfred Williams was not noticeably the last, only one of the most recent, of our peasant-poets.

But about the delayed birth of untutored expression in verse Southey has much that is interesting to say, and the distinctions that he draws have also been accepted in this book.

The distinction between the language of high and low life could not be broadly marked, till our language was fully formed, in the Elizabethan age: then the mother tongue of the lower classes ceased to be the language of composition; that of the peasantry was antiquated, that of the inferior citizens had become vulgar. It was not necessary that a poet should be learned in Greek and Latin, but it was that he should speak the language of polished society.

It would be a separate study, with these premises, to trace the uneducated poet in periods before the English Renaissance. Caedmon, who might otherwise be held to be not only the first poet, but the first peasant-poet, in the English tongue, could not be considered to be a forerunner of this tradition. When the cowherd of Whitby fell asleep in the stable and was visited by an angel who commanded him to sing of the beginning of created things, he certainly composed his songs in the language of low life. But the cleavage was between Latin and English, and during the course of centuries the vernacular was used, not as the antiquated language of the peasantry, but as a living and growing instrument of communication amongst all classes of society. As Southey indicates, it was not until the English language had developed sufficiently to absorb the traditional uses of Latin, and, during the seventeenth century, to have adopted within its structure that social division, once mirrored in two languages, between high and low life, not until then could the poetry of the educated and the uneducated be considered distinct.

During the eighteenth century, when the drift towards a mannered poetic style was most apparent, the attempts of those who were ignorant of this new *ars poetica* to jump the gap were most noticeable. The Romantics, Southey amongst them, considered that they had bridged it, and the "March of Intellect" was to bring with it a unified poetic medium which rich and poor could fashion in complete equality. Because he hoped there would be no need for further John Joneses, Southey declared such versifiers to be extinct.

Now, more than a century later, we are less confident than Southey of the direction that poetic expression will take; the peasant tradition is stranger to us than it was to him. But although we may seem to have lost sight of the main current we would be wise not to reiterate Southey's conclusion. If the stream of peasant poetry has gone to ground it is surely still quietly nourishing the roots of this generation's poetic achievement.

The Annals of the Poor

Sheer plod makes plough down sillion shine.

GERARD MANLEY HOPKINS: *The Windhover*

Since the Renaissance England has never been a country where the peasant was a segregated or distinct unit of society. The break-up of the manorial system and the introduction of the Enclosure Acts saw an end to the concept of sufficiency amongst small, independent units of the community. The pursuit of profits from the land was the natural outcome of greater internal security and the growth of trade under Tudor rule. It was inevitable that employer and employee became synonymous with rich and poor. Nevertheless enclosure did not follow swiftly after the break-up of the mediaeval farm. Not until the beginning of the nineteenth century could the peasant claim to be a disinherited and landless labourer. An effective class-merger was formed by the numerous yeomen-farmers of "forty-shilling freeholds." In Elizabethan times there were few social barriers to prevent free intercourse and interchange between the classes. Jealousies and snobbery had not sprung up, and a spirit of independence and franchisement moved amongst even the poorest of men.

The age was not without its injustices and discontentments. In East Anglia, where enclosure was more quickly effected than in many other areas, feeling ran particularly high. Kett's rebellion in 1548 showed that grievances even on agrarian matters were never completely stilled. Despite such local restlessness the agricultural labourer experienced during the late sixteenth century the benefits, unique until recent times, of having enough to eat and a modicum more. Labour was sufficiently scarce for men to be able to demand a living wage, and as four-fifths of the population was, at this time, engaged in agriculture there was less support than might have been expected for Levellers.

It is astonishingly difficult to assess with any fairness the conditions prevailing amongst the workers in rural England during the sixteenth and seventeenth centuries. The evidence is not so much conflicting as ill-tuned to present-day standards. An historical approach enables the twentieth-century reader to appreciate the hardships and discomforts of the Elizabethan labourer's life more poignantly than he himself, not blessed with foresight, would ever have imagined himself to have suffered. Overcrowding, lack of sanitation, unappetizing and meagre food were commonplaces not originally confined to the peasantry, and were not so much endured as expected. In winter the clay and wattle cottages of the farm-workers were often ill-heated and afforded poor protection against the weather. Children worked alongside their parents just as soon as they could be gainfully employed, and when old age incapacitated the labourer a haphazard system of poor relief barely gave him the security of subsistence. By the end of the seventeenth century one-fifth of the entire population of this island was reliably estimated to be in occasional receipt of alms.

Such a picture of misery, back-breaking toil and destitution can be gleaned from numerous sources and be held to represent the true condition of the peasantry even at a time of relative prosperity. It is not entirely false. Agriculture is, and always has been, the most exacting of occupations. The farmer works on the brink of disaster and his waking life is dedicated to his craft. The labourer whom he employed was lucky if he had the independence of a cottage and, in Harrison's words, "an acre of ground assigned to him whereon to keep a cow and set cabbages, radishes, parsneps, carrets, melons, pompons or such-like stuffe." More often he was dependent on the farm not only for his meals and wages but for the shelter of a stable or outhouse where he could spread his palliasse at night.

A day-labourer's wage was in itself insufficient to support a family, and as it was usually partly received in kind there was little that could be spared for the luxury of books and education. The two or three pounds that he might earn during the year were easily absorbed in maintaining a semblance of that well-being that Defoe detected amongst the English labouring poor, who "eat and drink, especially the latter, three times as much in value as any sort of foreigners of the

16

same dimensions in the world." Doubtless the European peasantry was undernourished, but Defoe's picture was rosy with the recollection of wakes and harvest-homes—red-letter days that enlivened a long year's toil. At festival time there was no stinting or restraint. There was food and drink in plenty, and a people more adept than ourselves in entertaining each other put hunger and hardship aside on their occasional gaudy nights. These brief, convivial interludes have served as working models for a golden age amongst those who knew nothing of the toil that earned them. Those who have examined more minutely the social structure of the times are equally prone to forget that limitation of desire bred a contentment that a shearing or harvest festival might crown with ample happiness.

Enclosure, bringing insecurity to the landless peasant by depriving him of his common rights, was an essential precursor to agricultural development throughout England, and the squirearchy who succeeded the feudal lords as principal property-holders became increasingly anxious to adopt a system of rural economy that was both efficient and profitable. It became possible to exploit the land, and wealth could be harvested and sheared beyond mere livelihood.

Gradually and unevenly an increased prosperity touched all classes of country dwellers during the sixteenth and seventeenth centuries. But there was more distinction between rich and poor; the smallholder without his common rights became a day-labourer, and the hierarchy of master and man became more rigidly defined. As the standard of living rose and a Poor Law (that, unsatisfactory as it was, remained virtually unaltered from 1601 to 1834) ensured a parish responsibility for its own paupers, so the necessity to work the land more profitably increased. Experience was codified, first by Fitzherbert with his *Boke of Husbandrye* in 1534, and then by Mascall, Harrison and others, not least of whom was Thomas Tusser.

"Good, honest, homely, useful old rhymes," Southey commented three centuries after Tusser had collected together and published his *Five Hundred Points of Good Husbandry*. He would have wished no better praise. But although he was country-born and claimed gentility from his East Anglian forebears Tusser's early life was spent not on the land but on the fringes of society and the Court. It was his singing voice that gained him an entrance first to St. Paul's and then to Eton, where he received instruction from the great Nicholas Udall himself. From Eton he went to Cambridge, and for ten years thereafter he was employed in some musical capacity at Court. It was only after his marriage and retirement that he returned to the eastern counties, and became an ambitious but unsuccessful farmer.

Tusser was a gentleman-farmer, but one whose interests lay in cultivating his own land and establishing a close, well-defined working relationship between master and man. Once agricultural method had been established this function was largely given over to the bailiff or overseer, the squire himself being less concerned with the routine and more with administration and the pursuit of pleasure. The squirearchy that men in Tusser's position moulded and imposed on the English country scene cannot but be familiar in its eighteenth-century guise. In its formative years, when new practices were being tried and the science of agriculture painfully learnt, it is less well known.

Farming in East Anglia was more advanced in its methods than almost anywhere else in the country at this time, due largely to the quick spread of enclosure there. Tusser himself was wholly in favour of this development, although he realized (remembering Kett's rebellion eight years before) that

> The poor at enclosures do grutch,
> Because of abuses that fall;
> Lest some man should have but too much,
> And some again nothing at all.

It is abundantly clear from the example of Tusser's "rym dogerel" quoted above that such verse adds nothing except, perhaps, a jingle-memorability to a sentiment that might have been more succinctly expressed in prose. Tusser was never a poet. His rhymes have a uniform, monotonous beat. Sense yields to circumlocution, inspiration to information, but the inflexible rhythm never alters. Every one of the five hundred points that a good husbandman needed to bear in mind, and many admonitions directed to the housewife too, are hammered into the memory regardless of the craftsmanship of verse or the beauty of language. Tusser pursues a purely didactic course, and remembering, perhaps, how the *Distichs of Cato* had, with their imperious hexameters, captured his unwilling memory as a child, he determined that an equally strong rhythm should impress his farming disciples—often semi-literate themselves—and plant his principles in their minds.

The advice was good, but Tusser himself never profited greatly from it. Fuller, who celebrated his modest fame in *The Worthies of Essex*, summed up his achievements.

He was successively a musician, schoolmaster, serving man, husbandman, grazier, poet; more skilful in all than thriving in any vocation. He traded at large in oxen, sheep, dairies, grain of all kinds, to no profit. Whether he bought or sold, he lost . . . . He spread his bread with all sorts of butter, yet none would stick thereon.

Tusser was not a peasant-poet. Indeed, but for the fact that he rhymed out of his experience (the phrase is Walter Blith's) he would have no claim to be remembered in this book. But experience is important, and is perhaps the greatest distinguishing feature in the verse of the numerous poorly-educated countrymen who fill these pages. Tusser knew what he was writing about, and gracelessly as he might express it his conscious instruction was not dissimilar in spirit from the grave and accurate descriptions of agricultural affairs written by the country poets of the eighteenth century.

Change and innovation crept slowly through the agrarian community. Centuries might pass before a common practice in the southern counties became generally adopted throughout England. Stubbes in the sixteenth century was not the first, nor was Barnes in the nineteenth the last, to protest against the slow extinction of common rights. Open field cultivation, a legacy from the manorial system of agriculture, was equally slow to disappear. Although in the East Anglia of Tusser's day "champion" country had largely given place to "severall," when Townshend and Coke of Norfolk were demonstrating at the beginning of the nineteenth century still newer ways towards agricultural improvement, there were large areas in the Midlands where strip cultivation was still commonly practised.

Over the slow evolution of his own destiny the peasant himself had no control. For the most part neither he nor his employer realized that their parochial actions formed part of a broader pattern to increase the riches of the land, its owners, and eventually, not without delays and injustices, of the workers themselves. That a gradual change was taking place in rural areas became increasingly apparent to those who, like Goldsmith, could look back to the days when "every rood of ground maintain'd its man." It was obvious that as the centuries advanced riches were accumulating, but that they were in any way to benefit those who toiled for them seemed hardly probable to the inhabitants of "sweet Auburn." No peasant voice spoke or was heard, no assistance or sympathy was offered. The cleavage between land-owners and landworkers became complete. Only one strength was left to the labourer: the broader dissemination of education. Only one chance of immediate advancement: patronage through the Arts.

In some measure education must precede self-expression. Even an oral tradition of poetry such as Bardism relied on the assimilation of a cultured heritage of song. The stimulus that might be provided by some wandering Autolycus could never be exploited without access to, and ability to comprehend, the written word. Before books were produced at a price not utterly prohibitive the labourer had no chance to develop a literary talent or to express himself in any but transient ways. Of the least formally educated poets in the centuries before Duck, Langland received a clerical, and Taylor a grammar-school education. The ordinary peasant could not obtain even this elementary grounding.

The development of peasant poetry was aided by a variety of dis-connected events. Amongst these were the spread of charity schools in rural areas (Duck was one of the first pupils), the improvement in communications which had hitherto physically isolated the country-dweller from cultural influences, and the repeal of the Licensing Act, which enabled printers to start businesses in the smaller towns through-out the country, and to print what they wished without fear of the consequences. Before the beginning of the eighteenth century master printers were limited in number to twenty, and apart from the two University Presses were wholly concentrated in London.

Very little printed matter and far less poetry, therefore, came into the hands of the countryman, and the cost deterred those whom the rarity had not already foiled. The Bible and the broadside were alpha and omega to the most aspiring peasant. Some squires, some parsons, and some independent landowners read and possessed books; the peasantry, still numbering about one-half of the population of this island, knew poetry only as they heard it in church, and practised it only as Dorothy Osborne overheard, when she walked "out into a common that lies hard by the house where a great many young wenches keep sheep and cows and sit in the shade singing of ballads."

Such, briefly, is the background of rural England before the eighteenth century in so far as it affected peasant poetry. During that time no man born and bred as a tiller of land succeeded in overcoming the difficulties of his occupation and writing in verse. Many great spirits rose from the meanest employments and assumed leadership in various walks of life, and in poetry a number of forceful and vigorous men made their voices heard despite disadvantages of birth and wealth. It is tempting to digress for a moment to consider at least one of these townsmen whose ambition was stimulated to pursue the Muse.

An ebullient zest for living and a flair for scribbling were the marks of John Taylor, a man meanly born whose occupation as a ferryman on the Thames earned him the title of the Water Poet. His collected works form a circumstantial and copious chronicle of the times. They were the product of little formal education but a great deal of acute and inquisitive observation on the pageantry of life around him.

> No learning but the Book of Nature,
> No academical poetic strains
> But homespun medley of my motley brains.

To no other age could Taylor, with his strangely mixed characteristics, have been so suited. A braggadocio and a familiar, a dare-devil and a wit; boyish in his enthusiasms, unrefined in his pleasures, yet equally one who could say with sincerity

> I *care* to get good books, and I take heed
> And *care* what I do either write or read;
> Though some through ignorance, and some through spite,
> Have said that I can neither read nor write.

21

But though my lines no scholarship proclaim,
Yet I at learning have a kind of aim;
And I have gathered much good observations,
From many human and Divine translations.

The little that is now remembered of John Taylor's life is mostly connected with the wagers he undertook and won; of how he walked to Prague, and attempted to sail down the Thames in a paper boat with two dried fish fastened to canes instead of oars (an expedition accomplished in thirty-six hours despite the fact that the paper disintegrated and only eight small bladders kept his craft afloat). Men could still live by their wits in Taylor's day and receive patronage that was not bestowed like charity. It was not necessary to be a social climber in order to converse with Ben Jonson in an ale-house, nor was it considered unusual to be the guest of nobility when one's employment was to scull passengers across the Thames. The pursuit of knowledge was venerated for its own sake; a century later the fields of study had expanded to require leisure (and consequently gentility) for even specialized learning.

The day of the talented amateur, the naturally cultivated man, was already on the wane. Taylor was an unabashed, enthusiastic amateur. He possessed one quality unique amongst the uneducated poets with which these pages are more specifically concerned—self-assurance. His character was strong and buoyant, and his verse, despite its lack of poetic merit, has a robust quality that one never finds amongst the diffident professional productions of Duck, Bloomfield, or Clare. No English rural poet has possessed an emphatic quality of expression so crude yet so compulsive. "We went into the house of one John Pinners," Taylor relates,

A man that lives amongst a crew of sinners,
And there eight several sorts of ale we had
All able to make one stark drunk, or mad.

The poetry is thin, it is the man behind it that we see; the Water Poet himself "in his habit as he lived." We are never able to penetrate the formality of self-expression that concealed the writers of *The Thresher's Labour* or *The Farmer's Boy*. Although their poems were conceived autobiographically and have considerable verisimilitude they were

22

unable to lure their readers into direct and active participation in the proposed subject. After the seventeenth century it became an ability more common in prose than in poetry. Taylor, "a literary bargee," as the *Dictionary of National Biography* succinctly terms him, had this one talent both in his life and in his works, a power to create personal interest. "There was a ship, quoth he."

Southey, whose sympathetic delight in the lowly and neglected poets of former days makes him in many respects the "onelie begetter" of this present book, sums up Taylor's achievements in his prefatory remarks to the poems of John Jones, an old servant.

If the Water Poet had been in a higher grade of society, and bred to some regular profession, he would probably have been a much less distinguished person in his generation. No spoon could have suited his mouth so well as the wooden one to which he was born. His way of life was best suited to his character, nor could any regular education so fully have brought out the sort of talent which he possessed. Fortunately, also, he came into the world at the right time, and lived in an age when Kings and Queens condescended to notice him, nobles and archbishops admitted him to their table, and mayors and corporations received him with civic honours.

It is always dangerous and often prejudicial to let a poet's performance be dependent for judgment upon the circumstances of his life. An uneducated poet, critically isolated and treated as a phenomenon distinct from his more fortunate contemporaries, may assume an unwarranted importance before the world. The old dispute about the relevance of a man's biography when considering his works was never more accentuated than in the study of uneducated poets. But the majority of readers will tend to agree with Johnson's conclusions when he discussed this problem in connection with his study of Shakespeare.

Every man's performances, to be rightly estimated, must be compared with the state of the age in which he lived, and with his own particular opportunities; and though to the reader a book be not worse or better for the circumstances of the author, yet as there is always a silent reference of human works to human abilities, and as the enquiry, how far man may extend his designs, or how high he may rate his native force, is of far greater dignity than in what rank we shall place any particular performance, curiosity is always busy to discover the instruments, as well as to survey the workmanship, to know how much is to be ascribed to original powers, and how much to casual and adventitious help.

Granted the pertinence of this tenet to the present work, it is incumbent on the critic to gratify any curiosity that may be aroused, first of all concerning the circumstances under which certain peasants were inspired to write poetry ("the instruments" in Johnson's disquisition), and secondly from a general critical standpoint to assess the value of this verse in relation to the poetic output of the age—that is "the workmanship."

Before beginning it is suitable to ask why these scattered and forgotten poets should be considered under the generic term peasant-poets, and what qualities make their work distinct or remarkable.

In his poem *O Dreams, O Destinations*, Mr. C. Day Lewis has the lines,

> Looking beyond, or backward, more and more
> We grow unfaithful to the unique minute
> Till, from neglect, its features stale and blur.

The simplest apology for the peasant-poet is that on such occasions he will be invariably faithful to "the unique minute." When nostalgia or artifice divert the stream of poetry from the record of sensory perception the uneducated poet will be lost. His will be a limited but constant talent, valuable not so much in itself as in its resuscitative power. In their way Duck and Bloomfield (or in our own times Alfred Williams and the Spanish shepherd-poet Miguel Hernandez) are the mouthpieces of external nature; touchstones of jasper that betray the gold in other men. Their imagery is timeless. Duck threshing, Burns ploughing are archetypal symbols to which sooner or later all poetry refers.

In English poetry no period has been more consciously "unfaithful to the unique minute" than the Augustan. It was not neglect but a studied narrowing of the field of vision that so delicately blurred the features of external nature. Before 1735, John Nixon declared,

> no Bard adorn'd our Isle,
> To celebrate the glorious sylvan Toil;

but it is with some surprise that we learn that it was Somerville, the author of *The Chase*, who repaired this deficiency. To our eyes this is just what Somerville did not do, for his is an essentially aristocratic

poem and avowedly celebrates those rural pursuits that are "too costly
for the Poor." This would in no way, however, conflict with Nixon's
argument. "The glorious sylvan Toil" was not intended to include
those labours in which Stephen Duck had so recently been engaged.
It was a periphrasis for the English Arcady that had been superimposed
on the countryside by a generation of Augustan poets, book-learned
and town-bred.

The outward manifestations of Augustan nature-poetry are too
familiar to need detailed examination. External nature became enmeshed in the pastoral tradition, and a poetic code of behaviour
circumscribed those writers who took their subjects from the woods
and fields. Pope, in his *Discourse on Pastoral Poetry*, was one of the
earliest and most influential exponents of this neo-classical art. A
Pastoral was, he declared, by definition, "an imitation of the action of
a shepherd, or one considered under that Character"; the setting
should be that Golden Age, long fabled by the poets of antiquity,
where men lived in innocent happiness, without labour, injustice or
strife. In order to make such compositions not only "delightful" but
true to their own conceit, the shepherds who were placed in these
surroundings had to be transfigured, and only the best side of their
life exposed. Verisimilitude suffered under such restrictions; indeed,
but for one saving clause all resemblance might have been lost. "Nothing more conduces to make these composures natural, than when some
Knowledge in rural affairs is discovered." Belatedly, perhaps even
grudgingly, but nevertheless as an unavoidable clause in the *fiat*, the
pastoral poet was referred to the countryman in order that a gloss of
reality might temper his contrivances.

The pastoral poems of the eighteenth century have many beauties
that do not concern us here; they were often the product of much
skill and ingenuity, but they were far removed from the life and
occupations of the labouring poor. Even the *Idylls* of Theocritus which
were revered as the grand originals of this form of writing were considered "perhaps too much inclining to rusticity." There were pro-
prieties that had to be observed by all writers of pastorals and only
Virgil was admitted to be beyond criticism.

Neither personal, introspective contemplation nor curious, scientific

25

enquiry had intruded upon the limpid detachment of the Augustan pastoral scene. Good sense, correctness of expression and lofty sentiment dominated the genre. Even Thomson whose influence, direct or indirect, upon the nature-poets of succeeding generations was incalculable, desired that such poetry should "exchange her low, venal, trifling subjects for such as are fair, useful and magnificent." A direct and accurate transfer of the sense-impression of the poet to the reader, without regard to the heightening power of symbolism or analogy, made it imperative that the subject to be recorded was (in the case of a lowly profession) viewed under the ideal conditions of a Golden Age, "when the best of men followed the employment." When Burns's plough turned up a mouse's nest in 1785 he was not constrained in drawing his parallels by the consideration that the affairs of mice reflected no credit onto the affairs of men.

The countryside of the pastoral was a neo-classical dream far removed from the work of the poets considered in this book; but by developing the art of landscape-gardening men of refined sensibility ensured that at least in the vicinity of their own homes natural features might be modified to conform to rules of taste, and thereby "the negligence of nature, wide and wild" could be kept at bay. Even these islands of good taste were tedious to the town-dweller, as Lord Ogleby in *The Clandestine Marriage* discovered, and amongst poets, who in order to get patronage and publishers had congregated in London, the countryside held few inherent charms. To leave London presupposed a lack of funds or wit, or possibly it might be to hide after an indiscretion.

> Whene'er a Courtier's out of place,
> The country shelters his disgrace,

declared Gay, and Pope, describing a visit to the intellectual desert that lay beyond Twickenham, tells how a young lady

> went to plain-work, and to purling brooks,
> Old-fashion'd halls, dull aunts, and croaking rooks.

Such a landscape was certainly not Arcadian, and it is scarcely to be expected that its inhabitants should occupy themselves as did the goatherds of Sicily. Few comedies for a century after the Restoration could resist the opportunity of a visit to the homes of the barbarous squirearchy amid their rural demesnes, but no one was interested in the peasantry who worked under them;

> Let rustic sports engage the lab'ring hind,
> And cultivated acres plough his mind,
> Let him to unfrequented woods repair,
> And snuff, unenvy'd, his lean mountain air.

A great deal of such comment was satirical, and Gay in *The Shepherd's Week* satirized the satirists by being completely straight-faced about even the most workaday aspects of country life. The wisdom of the old shepherd Cloddipole, for instance, is gravely exemplified:

> He first that useful secret did explain,
> That pricking corns foretold the gath'ring rain.

If Gay had written his introductory *Proeme* as a serious thesis and been interpreted by his readers in this way he would head the list of bene-factors to the cause of the peasant-poet; but like Matthew Arnold in Sir Max Beerbohm's cartoon his grin destroys any illusions of gravity. "It behoveth a Pastoral to be, as nature in the country affordeth," Gay wrote, and went on to profess his intention "to describe aright the manners of our own honest and laborious plough-men." As the *Proeme* continues both the axe and the grindstone become increas-ingly apparent. Not without reason Gay had taken offence at the number of indifferent imitations that had followed the publication in 1709 of Pope's *Pastorals*. "A rout and rabblement of critical galli-mawfry hath been made of late days by certain young men of insipid delicacy, concerning I wist not what, *Golden Age*, and other outrageous conceits, to which they would confine Pastoral." There was no reason, Gay points out, for such artifice; Theocritus himself had used language far from refined. The poems that he proposed to submit to the public were composed with no such pretensions but would describe the rural scene "just as thou mightest see it, didest thou take a walk into the fields at the proper season."

In Gay's pastorals we find a union between the revered ideal and the despised actual for the first time; but the effect in his poems and in those of his imitators—Somerville, for example—was not to promote better understanding of the country, or to rebuild a healthier tradition in the idiom, but to continue as an intellectual five-finger exercise with the old joke.

If the inhabited and cultivated landscape received little respect from the town-bred writers of the early eighteenth century the wilder prospects of mountain and heath were looked on with an emotion not far removed from fear. The descriptive word for such scenery was at its kindest "irregular," and more often "misshapen" or "monstrous." Richard Wilson, probably the greatest English landscape painter of the eighteenth century, received little popularity or praise for his work. The mournful grandeur of the high hills that he depicts, despite a classical precision of outline, was out of sympathy with the times. We need only dip into the works of Evelyn and Addison or read the journals of those temerarious enough to cross the Alps to discover why.

A similar horror afflicted those who contemplated "gloomy winter's inauspicious reign." The Augustans were fair-weather poets and hated to contemplate the ruffles on either the face of nature or their own delicately-wrought culture. During the course of the century this loathing of the darker aspects of nature underwent a sea-change. The reluctant welcome that Thomson extended to the "kindred glooms" and "cogenial horrors" of winter was mellowed over the years into the ubiquitous, Wordsworthian, "appetite, a feeling and a love." The reasons for this change were numerous, and some—the most germane to this study—will be examined in more detail in a few pages.

Dryden, so powerful a force in shaping the attitude of poets of the succeeding generation, was in some measure responsible for the indecision with which the Augustans approached external nature. It was axiomatic that a young poet should be familiar with classical literature; but the lessons he was encouraged to learn from Virgil and Theocritus could not endure unimaginative transplantation. Only under the guidance of these two precentors, however, does Dryden allow that his young poet

> without shame, may condescend
> To sing of gardens, fields, of flowers, and fruit.

Permission is grudgingly and reluctantly given, and before a word has been written an order of precedence has been set up. First in importance are the masters of antiquity, next their disciple the young poet, and lastly the subject itself, or rather that part of a broader subject that could be relied on to fit into a soothing and harmonious pattern in what Vernon Lee in *Euphorion* aptly describes as "the vague spring of gentlefolk."

In so far as Nature was seriously considered at all it was as a moral repository, and as neither imagination nor experience could extend the range of such didacticism the few natural images that were employed soon became blunted with much use. But the similitude, if neatly expressed, was relatively unimportant before the message which it carried. To an Augustan way of thinking it was an additional strength rather than a weakness if by an established circumlocution or a stereotyped phrase some aspect of the countryside could be tamed for use in polite society. Within the gates of the park Corydon might watch over his fleecy charge: beyond, a shepherd could graze sheep and no man of culture would deign to notice him. The peace of the Augustans was based on discipline and self-confidence; if the urchin, Nature, strayed into the drawing-room and could not be smartened up for company, he was turned out and quickly forgotten.

A generalization, especially about a period in literary history whose weakness lay in an inability to be specific, must not pass without some mention of those men and women who, either intentionally or by chance, groped their way towards a more perfect interpretation of the countryside around them. Thomson himself had such a profound effect on the writings of uneducated poets for a century after the publication of *The Seasons* that his work calls for separate consideration. But Thomson did not stand completely alone amongst his contemporaries as a faithful chronicler of country scenes, nor were his countrymen, the Scots, entirely responsible for the reawakening of interest in external nature amongst English poets. Before either *The Seasons* or Allan Ramsay's arcadian romance *The Gentle Shepherd*, which brought freshness and life to the time-worn pastoral theme, Lady Winchilsea was turning wistfully from the witty and malicious town to the delicate, unassertive beauty of her country seat.

> Oh, for my groves, my country walks, and bow'rs,
> Trees blast not trees, nor flow'rs envenom flow'rs.

In all her poetry, even in *A Nocturnal Reverie* which Wordsworth found to contain new images of external nature, she preserves a detachment, a spectator's attitude, which is not surprising when one considers how sheltered was an aristocratic existence and how few would be the opportunities for active participation in the life of the land. Her night wanderings seem to have had for Lady Winchilsea all the forlorn brilliance of a forbidden pleasure.

> Poets, wild as thou, were born,
> Pleasing best when unconfin'd,

she confided *To the Nightingale*. Anne Finch, Countess of Winchilsea, could never herself be so free. She who was first to choose the land as her subject was least at liberty to understand it as she wished. Only "whilst tyrant man does sleep" could she commune with the quiet world of nature, "when curlews cry beneath the village walls."

John Philips was another poet of the early eighteenth century whose largely unmemorable and didactic work *Cyder* is occasionally made vivid by some lovingly-observed description taken from life. Philips was one of the first poets to find a positive pleasure in mountainous country; not so much because under these conditions Nature could best "instruct our wandering thought" (Dyer, we suspect, climbed Grongar Hill, and Denham a century before had certainly ascended Cooper's Hill, for such a purpose) as for the simple pleasure afforded by the scene itself.

> Nor are the hills unamiable, whose tops
> To heaven aspire, affording prospect sweet
> To human ken.

A third poet who may serve to show that a genuine interest in the countryside was not wholly dead is John Dyer. A Welshman and bred, as Thomson was, in rural surroundings, it was natural (one is tempted to say inevitable) that his earlier poems such as *Grongar Hill*, possessed a freshness that the ponderously didactic verse-manual on sheep that he wrote towards the end of his life lacked. Even if the reader is not entirely convinced that it was for no better reason than to hear the thrush singing that the poet mounted so high, the expedition was one which pleased the author, and some of his enthusiasm—a quality sadly lacking in the prevalent moral-nature and neo-pastoral strains—is conveyed to the reader.

Dyer is said to have composed *Grongar Hill* when he was only sixteen, and this would bear out a general tendency during the early part of the century by which young poets born in country districts wrote their first poems with a sensitive feeling toward nature, based on their own experience, but after their inevitable migration to society and the town speedily lost these qualities and composed didactic and dramatic works instead. Even Thomson, who wrote *The Seasons* before he was thirty, ended his literary career with a succession of tragedies. It was seemingly impossible for a poet to know both Nature and the world of literature and fashion. Neither Duck nor Bloomfield succeeded.

There are no clear-cut reasons to account for the gradual change that took place during the length of the eighteenth century in the attitude of both poets and their public to external nature. A number of factors, varying in importance, deserve at least to be mentioned.

The general increase in educational facilities, especially in country districts, led to a certain cultural decentralization, and improvements in agricultural methods brought an increase of wealth and prosperity, especially to the landowning class of the community. Means of communication also improved; the state of the roads and the conditions of travel had not previously encouraged purposeless wandering. But Dr. Johnson, who often enjoyed a coach journey, appreciated the company rather than the external allurements of the countryside. It was not until later in the century (if we except such indomitable travellers as Celia Fiennes) that the Tour, undertaken for the express purpose of observing natural phenomena different from those to which one had been accustomed, became common. Arthur Young, whose lengthy and enthusiastic descriptions of several such expeditions did much to popularize them, was first amongst many (including Robert Bloomfield) who made the beauty and strangeness of their own countryside part of the common reading of those who stayed at home.

More important than these social developments were the changes that took place within the world of letters itself. The primitivist movement that sprang up within the Augustan camp was the most noticeable. A rude, barbaric, but nevertheless splendid heritage in our literary past had never been completely overlooked. Dryden adapted Chaucer; Addison reminded his readers of *Chevy Chase*. But when Percy issued his *Reliques of Ancient English Poetry* in 1765 a graceful tribute to dead antiquity was transformed into homage for a living tradition. During the same decade MacPherson gave to a willingly credulous public the turbid heroic fragments that he ascribed to the Gaelic bard Ossian, and Chatterton found poetic inspiration in the Gothic splendour of St. Mary Redcliffe.

The connection between the enthusiastic return to songs of other days and the changing attitude towards external nature is not immediately apparent. Gray, a man of learning whose researches into the dim glories of the past were not frivolously undertaken, can best provide us with the link. To him the Bard, such a figure as dominates his own Pindaric Ode, was the grand original of all poetry: the divinely-inspired, primitive singer. Essentially it is a romantic conception, but one for which Homer equally well as Ossian could stand as precedent. Noble and heroic as was Gray's idea, it was obvious that a spontaneous oral gift of song was not being nurtured in eighteenth-century England. Insofar as perfection could be looked for in the poetry of the day it was in simplicity and rugged naturalness rather than in grace and good sense. The poetic ideal was consequently far nearer to external nature than heretofore, and the inspired singer needed to treat not the refinements but the first principles of life itself. Gray's Bard, his friend Mason's Caractacus, the heroes of Norse or Celtic mythology were the protagonists: giants amongst men whose nobility and untutored sensibility provoked an intoxicated fascination in many who were unused to strong draughts of romantic heroism.

Foremost amongst those who resisted the spell was Johnson. He doubted the authenticity of MacPherson's poems, was in no way stimulated by *Chevy Chase*, and found little truth to nature in the poetry of former days. "Mere obvious nature," he added, "may be exhibited with very little power of mind."

But enthusiasm for times past continued without abatement. The Gothic novel proved an immediate success, and genuine antiquarianism flourished. It became increasingly necessary to define with more precision that ideal society where simple greatness might yet be found, where men who combined the virtues of the heroes of old and the more recently appreciated arts of peace still lived. Gray, in *The Progress of Poetry*, started the search, and visited the frozen north and the little-known coasts of Chile

> to hear the savage youth repeat
> In loose numbers wildly sweet
> Their feather-cinctured chiefs, and dusky loves.

It was hopefully expected that uninhibited "loose numbers" might be the daily speech of such children of nature. There was less wonderment, therefore, and more encouragement if a peasant from one's own land broke into verse.

The quest but not the concept of the noble savage was originated by Gray. Florio and Spenser had used the idea, and it reappears in *Oroonoko*, who was himself "To Honour bound! and yet a Slave to Love!" The fact that Stephen Duck, who was not a deeply read man, chose to make his Amanda just such a noble, unselfish savage is some indication of the prevalence of the idea. Each new territory that was discovered brought with it some rumour of the natural man, and not only a Tahitan youth (whose manners, Fanny Burney declared, "shamed education") but a family of Eskimos were transported to London to see whether by chance they represented the great ideal. There is a suspicious similarity between the idyllic conditions under which the noble savage was expected to live and those prevailing in the Golden Age described in Pope's *Discourse on Pastoral Poetry*. The parallel, however, is not complete. Whereas the Augustan dream was of a sophisticated Arcady, the quest for the noble savage later in the century was grounded in the genuine belief that it was from lowly and untutored peoples that true greatness originated.

It was, perhaps, a reaction from the self-confidence of that which had gone before, certainly it was a state of mind reached independently of Rousseau, whose teaching scarcely touched England until nearly the turn of the century, that made many men who seemed to see the art of poetry and sensibility disappearing from their country search among the ashes for a new phoenix to rise. Some, like Goldsmith, looked inwardly to find why their own land did not produce greatness and found Auburn uninhabited.

> Ill fares the land, to hast'ning ills a prey,
> Where wealth accumulates, and men decay.

Others searched far afield for a new generative force, and received partial satisfaction in learning from the gentle and refined Tahitan, Omai, of a land where food grew on trees, where life was simply and happily lived, but where Ossian or the Bard would have been sadly out of place.

Some not insignificant, though entirely unconscious, allies in the general search for primitive inspiration were the English uneducated poets themselves. During the eighteenth century, following the example of Stephen Duck, they had multiplied, and some of them at least had obtained a considerable degree of temporary fame. It became almost a fashion amongst the patrons of letters to support at least one "untaught genius." Although few of these artisan and peasant-poets achieved a place in the halls of fame (we shall see something of their work in a later chapter), they did at least encourage the belief that poetry might, like Aeetes's dragon's teeth, spring fully armed from the earth. The benevolent tolerance that greeted the eccentricity of Stephen Duck when he turned poet was replaced half a century later by a determination that no poetic merit should escape unnoticed. Milkwomen, cobblers, pipe-makers were all paraded before the public—but even so William Blake was ignored.

Although the Augustans would never have admitted it, their attitude towards external nature was in one respect akin to the mediaeval. The eighteenth century that witnessed the steady growth of the scientific spirit—investigating the facts, and not confusing them with the spiritual meanings, of the world around them—was in revolt against the old distinction between a moral lesson which was important and could be inferred from phenomena that in themselves were not worth enquiring into, in favour of an impartial enthusiasm after

34

knowledge for its own sake. The moralization of nature, that did so much to capture man's escaping thoughts and reflect them back upon himself, died hard. Wordsworth himself was not entirely free from the habit, and probably the majority of poets have at one time or another harnessed the disinterested powers of Nature for their own moral purposes.

From the Stoics of ancient Greece to the present day a doctrine of detachment from, and independence of, the external world has recurred in man's thought. Nor has it been detachment alone that parted man and his environment. A sense of the unhelpfulness of Nature, and consequently of her inherent inferiority, puzzled even those who have been among her greatest admirers.

> On things inanimate we would force
> Some share of our divided grief,
> Whilst Nature (unconcern'd for our relief)
> Pursues her settled path, her fixt and steady course,

complained Lady Winchilsea; and as a corollary soothing to the hurt pride of man Emerson, many generations later, reiterated the old fallacy, "Nature is ancillary to man." Foremost amongst the poets who have felt no necessity to assert their superiority as human beings over the brute and inanimate creation are the peasants. An unself-conscious humility towards external nature, bred from the respect that close association often imparts, is one of the most distinctive features of this class of versifier: perhaps the only metaphysical link that can be said to exist between the diversely talented writers who fill this book. The same spirit may be seen in D. H. Lawrence's feeling towards external nature. The collier's son seemed to find so close an association with nature that it became a part of his living being. No other poet of his generation, however much he reported on the natural scene, achieved a comparable fusion of identity and sympathy in his descriptive writing.

Of all the causes that contributed to a gradual alteration in the attitude of the *literati* in eighteenth-century England towards external nature the most obvious, and probably the most influential, was the cumulative growth of new ideas within the literary world itself. The spirit of independent scientific investigation was becoming more and more popular. Bewick drew and Gilbert White described with meticulous care the living things around them. Crome and Gainsborough were teaching the public to look with unprejudiced eyes at an unpeopled landscape. But within literary circles the imitators and admirers of Thomson were making familiar to an increasingly enthusiastic public those simple, outdoor pleasures that had now been hallowed by a master touch. Long after their author was dead *The Seasons* acted as a leaven upon the literature of the century. It was the necessary authority; a hard core round which a snowball as it rolled along could grow. To the author of *The Seasons* we must turn next, for it is only through his work that we can interpret subsequent effusions from pens less trained and less influential than Thomson's own.

James Thomson:
The Vision and the Faculty

Delightful task! to rear the tender thought,
To teach the young idea how to shoot.

JAMES THOMSON: *Spring.*

It is well known that the publication of *The Seasons* caused the literary world of Thomson's day to look more directly and with more enthusiasm at its natural environment. Although lip-service had always been paid to nature, the word had become a term of art amongst a town-centred generation of poets; in view of the popularity of Thomson's poem it is hardly surprising that a mild but noticeable reorientation took place. It is less well known and more surprising that *The Seasons* also captured the imagination of those who knew the world of external nature intimately. For fully a century men such as Duck, Bloomfield, Clare and virtually every countryman in England who found expression in verse, acknowledged his indebtedness to *The Seasons.* At a time when rancour and obstinacy disturbed literary judgment Thomson escaped all serious detraction and gave immediate pleasure to many who had never been touched by poetry before.

As we have already seen, Thomson was not alone amongst poets in seeking to recapture the poetry of closely-observed landscape. But he was undoubtedly the most successful, the most whole-hearted and the most enthusiastic. Had he been propounding a novelty or a new departure in poetic tradition he could not have been so kindly treated, for innovation is never received without protest in any branch of the Arts. Although he was writing on a subject and in a manner different from the contemporary practice, he did not disturb old-established theories, but rather added to them by revealing new delights and broadening an existing vision. Thomson was not even an incipient

37

romantic. In literature as in life he was a neighbour and friend of Pope, but whereas Pope turned to the city for his pleasure and his prey Thomson was most happy under the beech-trees in Hagley Park.

Because he was not radical in his innovations, yet nevertheless succeeded in painting a tolerably accurate, objective picture of the rural year, Thomson was accepted in the country as well as in the town as the mouthpiece of external nature. Criticism was never levelled at him on a point of fact, though there are plenty of examples of wishful Arcadianism in his agricultural descriptions. Amongst townsmen there were few who had enough specialized knowledge to contradict him, whilst in the country doubtless the pomp and grandeur of Thomson's verse with its patina of wide learning impressed the ill-educated. It was the real countryside that flaunted its colours through *The Seasons*, a diffuse, usually unlocalized picture, but it was drawn from life, and drawn in an unselfconscious manner, of which only a Scot seemed capable at that time.

When Thomson went to the University at Edinburgh he found himself surrounded by a circle of young men as enthusiastic as any in London, not unknowledgeable about English books and literary trends, but bound to a tradition of their own as old as Gavin Douglas and never urbanized.

Thomson himself was a lowlander, born in 1700 the son of the minister of Southdean, a lonely and rugged parish with the river Jed flowing past the manse and the Cheviots rising behind. A childhood spent in such surroundings, the hillsides windswept and bare, the parishioners preoccupied in the struggle for bare livelihood and his own father struck dead in the act of exorcism, might understandably have coloured his later writings. Much of the lurid over-writing that occurs in *The Seasons* finds its roots in these early years. His florid vocabulary and derivative technique can also be ascribed to the lust for book-learning that was the hall-mark of an educated Scotsman. These are venial faults, for they are faults of enthusiasm, and it is that quality that lifts Thomson above the ruck of poets.

It is not surprising that, in 1724, before his theological studies were completed, Thomson travelled to London. Many young scholars from the north rounded off their education in London or one of the centres of learning on the Continent. But it is notable that he stayed on the fringe of the city all his life, without attempting to return to his native soil. His jobs as tutor to various noble houses did not inflict an exclusively town life upon him, and the softer, more gracious mode of living in the southern counties proved more sympathetic to his indolent nature than the harshness of the north. His theological calling was heard more faintly and at last merged into an unenquiring Deism that satisfied orthodoxy and brought the world of nature snugly into his cosmic plan.

If he had not spent his first months in London writing, as his compatriots Riccaltoun and Armstrong were writing, of winter landscapes and activities, and if his poem had not achieved success, it is doubtful if we should know of Thomson today. London would have blunted his senses and occupied his mind. He wrote *The Seasons* whilst memory was fresh and zeal was untempered by sloth. His employment aided him by the opportunities it gave of cultivating his taste for gardens and wandering on foot over the estates of his patrons. "This is the truly happy life," he wrote to Miss Elizabeth Young (whom he would doubtless have married had her mother consented) as he sat in Lord Lyttleton's park,

the union of retirement and choice society; it gives an idea of that which the patriarchal or golden age is supposed to have been . . . The country life with you, diversified now and then by the contrast of the town, is the wish of my heart.

With such a desire we may fully sympathize still, and to achieve such a well-modulated existence was the art of eighteenth-century country life.

Although he inherited and never lost a strong dialect and a carelessness of manner and dress (Shenstone declared he had nothing of the gentleman in him), Thomson dearly loved the cultivated moderation and elegance of the English landed gentry. When he crossed the Channel he declared that his Muse had not followed him, and although his imagination enabled him to describe, often with great vividness, incidents in Lapland or Cathay he was happiest when celebrating more homely scenes. Although he was not exactly a local poet it is not unfitting that Thomson should be most commonly remembered as the author of a patriotic song. On a larger canvas *The Seasons* is as much a national work as *Rule, Britannia*, and this aspect had particular charm to the uneducated landsman who felt the spell of his poetry.

Love of country is the most inbred of English emotions. An intellectual correlation of patriotism and scoundrels would have been incomprehensible to the majority of the poets in this book. Whatever ill-fortune or ill-treatment beset the common folk of Britain they never dreamt of blaming their country. The land was so much a part of them that loyalty to the island on which they lived was self-loyalty which only a spiritual persecution could persuade them to abandon. *The Seasons* appealed directly and objectively to a background of life which every reader acknowledged to be good.

Thomson was not concerned with the manifest discord and inequality of life; he never pretended to contemplate

> How many shrink into the sordid hut
> Of cheerless poverty.

The ruffled surface-waters of social and moral differences did not attract him. He dived deeper where the main currents flowed in broad, unchallenged streams. Crabbe, by contrast, chose an altogether different level for his poetry; he buffeted on the surface in the froth of controversy. But it was Thomson, whose truths were undisturbed by argument, who appealed most strongly to the countryman. The poetry of "should-be" and "might-have-been" has little attraction to the uneducated: the past is good for stories,

> For lewed peple loven tales olde,
> Swiche thynges kan they wel reporte and holde,

and the future is not worth speculating upon. It is the poetry of the familiar and verifiable present that the peasant will read and, if he can, write about. It is not always the best poetry, but it is either useful, like Tusser's rhymes, or inspiriting, like *The Seasons*.

Thomson wrote a true picture of external nature, but it is heightened (not falsified) in such a way that the reader is flattered at having shared in familiar glories, and resolves to appreciate them as fully by himself next time. The opening description in *Spring* of early ploughing is

40

an excellent example both of the buoyant and vivid quality of Thomson's verse and of the heightening of his subject that he employs.

> Joyous the impatient husbandman perceives
> Relenting Nature, and his lusty steers
> Drives from their stalls to where the well-used plough
> Lies in the furrow loosened from the frost.
> There, unrefusing, to the harnessed yoke
> They lend their shoulder, and begin their toil,
> Cheered by the simple song and soaring lark.

There is a conspiracy of well-being between the protagonists in this passage. Their labour has, for man and beast, a freshness and enthusiasm that captures the very essence of the season; but it is not strictly true. Thomson must often have seen the cattle released from the dark confinement of their winter quarters, weak and half-starved, and certainly not lusty enough to enter so vigorously into the spring ploughing.

This divergence between the spirit and the letter of descriptive writing which occurs so frequently in Thomson's poem and which cannot in all cases be attributed to Arcadianism, is neatly summarized by Mr. Stephen Spender in a recent essay on Shelley. "There is a divorce between art and actuality or, at any rate, a marriage in which the relationship between the two is governed by the realization that they deal with different kinds of reality." Thomson, who was writing objectively on a subject so familiar that it might easily have become prosaic, instinctively appreciated the truth of poetry that could be distilled from the truth of actuality. In this his strength and his endurance as a poet lies. Failure to recognize this dichotomy led many lesser descriptive writers to fetter their inspiration to their eyesight.

The objectivity of Thomson's natural descriptions has already been remarked on; as Hazlitt describes it, "he gives back the impression which the things themselves make upon us in nature." This quality is distinctive not only of *The Seasons* but of the age in which it was written. The reader of nature-poetry today has so strong a background of the romantic treatment of the subject that he might accuse Thomson of loss of opportunity or failure to clinch his argument in lines like the following:

41

> Thus the glad skies,
> The wide-rejoicing earth, the woods, the streams,
> With every life they hold, down to the flower
> That paints the lowly vale, or insect-wing
> Waved o'er the shepherd's slumber, touch the mind
> To nature tuned, with a light-flying hand
> Invisible.

But the passage requires no associative emotion to complete it. Thomson was describing the natural scene for its own sake; an universal, wide-sweeping picture without reference to man's inmost soul and being which such a statement might have mirrored in Wordsworth's imagination. Thomson never attempted to live nature, as did Clare. He was an interested but detached witness of the seasonal pageant, and saw in nature the praise of God, not an image of God Himself.

The technique of Thomson's poetry has been discussed by his critics more fully than his subject. Even his greatest admirers have admitted that his style is disconcertingly uneven. His blank verse had sufficient ease and fluency for Johnson himself to commend it, but the manner in which he fills his lines is unpredictable. There are times, as Macaulay has shown, when to read alternate lines does not detract from the sense; but equally there are periods of highly-charged, even condensed, poetic beauty. It is pleasant to remember the rapturous flux of words in which he tells of "the passion of the groves" (a passage that only *The Testament of Beauty* can equal), or when the birds are migrating in autumn to read

> Infinite wings! till all the plume-dark air
> And rude resounding shore are one wild cry;

but it is equally easy to scoff. Perhaps Thomson's "panting muse" laboured too consciously and too hard for effect; at all events he is read now with no predisposition to sympathy and little time to spare on the part of the general reader. New editions of *The Seasons* have not often appeared in this century—the reason may be found in the passage that follows, which seems to include a representative selection of Thompson's stylistic faults. The lines are taken from *Spring* and apostrophize the Universal Being.

By thee disposed into congenial soils,
Stands each attractive plant, and sucks and swells
The juicy tide—a twining mass of tubes.
At thy command the vernal sun awakes
The torpid sap, detruded to the root
By wintry winds, that now in fluent dance
And lively fermentation, mounting, spreads
All this innumerous-coloured scene of things.

It would be ponderous to dwell upon the curiosities of this passage were it not for the profound effect that such writing had upon the serious and impressionable disciples who succeeded Thomson. A poem which was to be the *vade mecum* of a century of landsmen could not fail to impress its characteristics upon many of them. We shall find imitators—usually bad imitators—of Thomson's turgid loquacity, his neologisms, his inevitable qualifying adjective, his over-writing and his circumlocutions, writing in the magazines and hopefully publishing pamphlets of verses throughout the rest of the century. Very few of these rhymers succeeded in capturing any of Thomson's descriptive strength, but however unsuccessful their emulation they had all at least read his poem.

The Seasons brought a spirit of tenderness, a new humanity, into eighteenth-century poetry. Thomson himself was even-tempered and phlegmatic by nature. He recognized and deprecated man's cruelty to man wherever he found it, praising prison-reform and decrying the over-rigorous collection of tithes after bad farming years. But it is the acute concern that he displays on behalf of animals and birds that distinguishes Thomson from his predecessors. In the previous century Izaak Walton—a kindly man by all accounts—gave a minute description of the manner in which live frogs should be impaled upon the hook as bait; Thomson, far from using frogs, implores the angler,

But let not on thy hook the tortured worm
Convulsive twist in agonizing folds.

His feeling towards the mute suffering of living things was not confined to fishing-bait. Wherever he saw birds caged, animals wounded or fish caught too young he was vocal in protest. He even challenged

43

the universally tolerated sport of hunting, and never participated himself. Thomson's humanizing tendencies, by which living creatures seem to plead their own cause through the very pathos of their portrayal in his pages, may have helped to form that national characteristic by which Englishmen are said to be distinguishable abroad—kindness to animals. Certainly during the course of the century the solicitude that countrymen had always displayed towards their horses and dogs spread to include those wild creatures that were not noxious to the community.

A poet who loves florid diction naturally inclines towards the dramatic and violent aspects of nature, and might neglect the violet hours when colours and textures are more subtle and less easy to define. This is partly true of *The Seasons*, and had Thomson relied entirely upon English agricultural life for his material he might have heightened the perils of storm and snow and expanded upon the joys of sun and shower to a ludicrous degree. But his long poem has a world-wide sweep; he visits all lands, speculates upon the stars in the sky and the ore in the earth. Like one of his beloved tempests when he seems to flag and search for words or suitable subjects it is only the prelude to a fresh foray into the inexhaustible treasure-house of the world. The poem itself seems to have captured something of the "negligence of Nature, wide and wild."

There is little that comes amiss to Thomson's fluent pen; the insignificant and the universal are given a dramatic gloss and jostle each other in print. Once again no countryman could fail to be impressed when sights and experiences familiar to him in his daily life were exalted by their proximity to the rich and rare. Thomson's lack of method would have worried such a man less than a trained critic. Johnson, for instance, complained of *The Seasons* that "the memory wants the help of order, and the curiosity is not excited by suspense or expectation."

The grand manner and a vision of the moral poet with his singing robes about him is never far distant from Thomson's most sylvan scene. On formal occasions, introductions, invocations, and philosophical reflections, he writes in a self-conscious and pontifical manner that must deter many readers. Such striving after grandeur would have seemed less intrusive in his own day, and was indeed an accepted

44

part of the machinery of a considered poem of this kind. There was always a moral to be drawn from nature, always a reference to human conduct in that self-conscious age. To the uneducated, however, there was magnificence in Thomson's manner (who would recognize a bad imitation of Milton here or there?) and instruction to be gained from his analogies. What could be more clear or commendable than the parable told after a description of summer insects on the vanity of human wealth?

> Thick in yon stream of light, a thousand ways,
> Upward and downward, thwarting and convolved,
> The quivering nations sport; till, tempest-winged,
> Fierce Winter sweeps them from the face of day.
> Even so luxurious men unheeding pass
> An idle summer life in fortune's shine. . . .

The moral is obvious, but it requires a good deal of space and much breath to follow Thomson through his digressions. He had no need to compress his meaning for succinctness was not so highly esteemed in verse as nowadays. But perhaps digression was a misnomer, for in effect these rambling, moral similes and sentimental, often inappropriate anecdotes are equally parts of the fabric of the poem, only they have faded more quickly with the passage of time.

In this brief survey many aspects of *The Seasons* and all consideration of Thomson's other works, notably *The Castle of Indolence*, have been neglected. This is intentional, as within the context of this book Thomson, who was neither an Englishman nor uneducated, has no direct part to play. Some justification for these pages will, it is hoped, be found in the chapters that follow. For nearly a century *The Seasons* was unchallenged as the authoritative picture of the English countryside. Thomson himself believed not only that his subject was one worthy of elevated treatment in verse, but that he had rendered it with fidelity. However much we may carp at his stylistic distortions, diffuseness and Arcadianism it cannot detract from the unqualified admiration that his poem elicited from those men most ready to judge facts—the barely literate countrymen of England. We would do well to doubt that Thomson was sternly prepared to overthrow the classical pastoral tradition,

> But now those white unblemished minutes, whence
> The fabling poets took their golden age,
> Are found no more amid these iron times,
> These dregs of life!

But despite his many classical affinities he never transported the Muse of Theocritus and Virgil lock, stock, and barrel to pine in the English woods and fields as many of his contemporaries had attempted to do. He effected a compromise that neither challenged the venerated monopoly of the classics, nor failed to satisfy those who looked first for circumstantial accuracy in poetry. The success of this union was Thomson's greatest achievement, and its result was noticeably to broaden the poetry-reading public of the land.

Stephen Duck

O You, MENALCAS, know my abject Birth,
Born in a Cot, and bred to till the Earth.

STEPHEN DUCK: *Gratitude*

The same year that Thomson completed *The Seasons* with the addition of *Autumn*, and apostrophized the

sound, unbroken youth,
Patient of labour, with a little pleased;
Health ever blooming, unambitious toil;
Calm contemplation, and poetic ease,

Stephen Duck, a tasker from Wiltshire, deserted these enviable pursuits for the greater felicity of preferment at Court. His name is now almost forgotten, and his verse unread, but the speed with which he rose from day-labouring at four and sixpence a week to become a candidate for the Laureateship did not pass unnoticed in 1730.

Duck was born in about 1705, the son of a labourer from Charlton in Wiltshire. He was more fortunate than most of his contemporaries in attending a Charity School, where he learnt to read and write, until he was fourteen years old. In the account of his life that prefaces the pirated edition of his works it is claimed "that he took his Learning too fast, even faster than the Master could give it him," and in consequence that he was removed from the school by his parents and set to the plough, lest he should become too fine a gentleman for his family to support. However this might be, Stephen enjoyed his schooling, but quickly forgot the little that he had learnt.

The Charity School movement, a development in the segregation of education that increased during the century, was instituted during the reign of Queen Anne. Duck was amongst the first to benefit from this form of teaching, though by the end of her reign 20,000

47

country children were attending Charity Schools. Had he been born in an earlier age and displayed those same precocious talents, he might well have been adopted and taught by some monastic order, or supported through a Grammar School and University education by a benevolent landlord. But during the eighteenth century there was an increasing reluctance to allow class barriers to be overridden. If a man was born to manual labour the analogy of breaking a horse to the collar young applied. To be a contented labourer it was considered a disaster to be literate. The apprenticeship to husbandry should be one of practical application.

> Accurs'd the man, whom fate ordains, in spite,
> And cruel parents teach, to Read and Write!
> What need of letters? Wherefore should we spell?
> Why write our names? A mark will do as well.

So Churchill argues, and Bernard de Mandeville, who claimed that in his day it was still possible for ambitious labourers to alter their social conditions by their own efforts, was nevertheless of the opinion that too much, rather than too little, was being done to assist them.

Charity Schools certainly brought a rudimentary education to a great number of people who had previously received none. But there was humiliation attached to their name and their conception, and less chance than ever of the brilliant few rising above the general mediocrity. Only in recent years has the concept of education for all men, regardless of their future employment, received any widespread support. Even Cobbett, a staunch champion of the rights of the downtrodden, defended the illiteracy of the agricultural worker, and as late as 1807 declared that those who laboured with their bodies neither desired to, nor should, work with their minds. Mandeville, whose cynical and outspoken views on education are voiced in his *Essay on Charity and Charity Schools*, expresses the views of the society in which Stephen Duck grew up.

To make the Society Happy and People Easy under the meanest Circumstances, it is requisite that great numbers of them should be Ignorant as well as Poor. Knowledge both enlarges and multiplies our Desires, and the fewer things a Man Wishes for, the more easily his Necessities may be supply'd.

The Welfare and Felicity therefore of every State and Kingdom, require that the Knowledge of the Working Poor should be confin'd within the Verge of their Occupations, and never extended (as to things visible) beyond what relates to their Calling. The more a Shepherd, a Plowman or any other Peasant knows of the World, and the things that are Foreign to his Labour or Employment, the less fit he'll be to go through the Fatigues and Hardships of it with Chearfulness and Content.

Reading, Writing and Arithmetick, are very necessary to those, whose Business require such Qualifications, but where Peoples Livelihood has on dependance on those Arts, they are very pernicious to the Poor, who are forc'd to get their Daily Bread by their Daily Labour. Few Children make any Progress at School, but at the same time they are capable of being employ'd in some Business or other, so that every Hour those of poor People spend at their Book is so much time lost to the Society. Going to School in comparison to Working is Idleness, and the longer Boys continue in this easy sort of Life, the more unfit they'll be when grown up for downright Labour, both as to Strength and Inclination. Men who are to remain and end their Days in a Labourious, Tiresome and Painful Station of Life, the sooner they are put upon it at first, the more patiently they'll submit to it for ever after.

In view of such sentiments it would have been small wonder if Duck's mother had been anxious lest Stephen should over-educate himself.

For three years the young man worked on a small-holding that his father had acquired, but when this project failed, and the farm had to be sold, Stephen hired himself out as a day-labourer. He still had "a longing after Knowledge," but it was not until he was nearly twenty and had married that he started to educate himself in earnest. This was no easy undertaking. A tasker's work, as he himself describes in his finest poem, *The Thresher's Labour*, started at dawn, and often did not end until after dark. Not only was there little time for study, but the wages he received allowed no margin for the purchase of books. From his master he could expect little sympathy, and even his wife failed to understand the driving spirit that made him work overtime in order to purchase three books of elementary mathematics. To her neighbours she confided "that her Husband dealt with the Devil, and was going mad because he did nothing all day but talk to himself, and tell his Fingers." A century later Sydney Smith might almost have had Duck in mind when he remarked, "Amongst the real inhabitants of the country, the reputation of reading and thinking is fatal to character."

The little that is known about the life of Stephen Duck we largely owe to an "Account of the Author," written in the form of a letter to a friend, by the Rev. Joseph Spence, Professor of Poetry at Oxford. This benevolent man was amongst the first to realize Duck's merits, and remained his close friend throughout life. Duck was not alone in receiving Spence's encouragement; Thomas Blacklock, the blind Scottish poet, and Robert Hill, the learned tailor, were both shepherded by Spence into the world of print. The enthusiasm with which such men as he and Capel Lofft helped the indigent poets of their generations ensured that the rural Muse was at least not stillborn, and that despite the widening class-cleavage a commonalty amongst the Arts might still be achieved.

Duck's self-education, Spence tells us, could scarcely have been carried on had he not had a companion, the possessor of a library of two or three dozen books, with whom he could talk and read. "They were perhaps equally well inclin'd to learn, both struggling for a little Knowledge; and, like a Couple of Rowers on the same Bottom, while they were only striving perhaps, which should outdo his Companion, they were really each helping the other, and driving the Boat on the faster."

The books that Duck and his "one Dear Friend" read together are an interesting reflection of the instinctive taste of an unsophisticated poet. It was too early for *The Seasons* to have found its way to Charlton; books "hot from the press" were not within Duck's power to buy. But Thomson's poem, that stimulated both Bloomfield and Clare to an awareness of poetry, did not pass unnoticed a few years later. In his *Description of a Journey* Duck is the first of a long line of country poets to pay tribute to Thomson's "bold, unfetter'd Lay." Duck's early reading was eclectic. "*Milton*, the *Spectators*, and *Seneca*, were his first Favourites," reports Spence, and in addition he had read several plays of Shakespeare, "some of *Epictetus*, *Waller*, *Dryden's Virgil*; *Prior*, *Hudibras*, *Tom Brown*, and the *London Spy*." Like Adam Eyre, the yeoman farmer from Yorkshire, who, half a century earlier, had left a record of his library and his opinions, Duck was drawn by the arguments of the Christian apologists; and Addison's *Defence of Christianity*, as well as the Bible itself, were high in his esteem.

Many of the books mentioned would seem indigestible fare for an ill-educated farm-hand. Spence comments that "the Pains he has taken for the Pleasure of improving himself, are incredible," and certainly to settle down after the labours of the day, to disentangle the beauty and meaning of Milton with the aid of Bailey's Dictionary and "a sort of an *English* Grammar," shows extraordinary perseverance. How often such diligence has met with no reward, how many mute, inglorious Miltons have searched in vain for a patron, it is idle to consider. But it is not impossible that Gray had Stephen Duck in mind when he wrote that line of the *Elegy*. Although he is forgotten now, "The Thresher, with all his defects" was considered by many of his contemporaries to have been "a superior genius to Mr. Pope." The chances against his discovery, together with the resemblance of Duck to Gray's own conception of the natural, untrammelled poet, could not have failed to impress the author of the *Elegy*.

Whereas *The Seasons* offers a model at once familiar and stirring to the peasant-poet, the poetry of Milton, august and unstooping in its aspiring flight, would seem too remote in language and experience to serve as a catalyst to a lowly Muse. It was *Paradise Lost*, however, that first gave Duck a high taste in poetry. "*Stephen* read it over twice or thrice with a Dictionary, before he could understand the Language of it thoroughly. . . . Indeed it seems plain to me, that he has got *English* just as we get *Latin*." In such circumstances it seemed all the more astonishing to Spence that he could understand not only the letter, but the spirit of the the poem, and had sufficient critical acumen to realize that his original draft of *The Shunammite* in Miltonic blank verse laboured under all the disadvantages, and possessed none of the grandeur, of his master's technique.

Although Milton was the touchstone of his poetry, it was not through him that Duck started to write. When he went out to work in the fields he would take a *Spectator* with him. By dint of harder work than his companions he would gain a half-hour's leisure whilst the others caught up with him. During this relaxation he would have time to read an essay. But there were disadvantages to this; "he us'd to sit down all over Sweat and Heat, without regarding his own Health." It was the occasional verses that filled up the odd spaces in the *Spectator* that first stirred Duck to emulation.

None of his early efforts is preserved. Like Clare's first verses they were no sooner written than burnt. It is improbable that we have lost anything of value by their destruction, but the nature of the verses that inspired such effusions is worth remarking on. Thomson and Milton made the minds of peasants receptive to poetic impulses, but the indifferent, or even bad, verse in newspapers and periodicals made them write. It is natural enough that even if a ploughboy-poet is not suffering from a sense of inferiority, he would prefer to compete with those whom he imagines he can rival or excel. Once he has broken silence the influence of the great masters of poetry may become painfully apparent in the peasant's work; but the credit for stirring the latent poetic impulse must go, at least in part, to a legion of forgotten poetasters.

With his eager thirst for knowledge and his ability to write verses, Duck soon became parochially noticeable; but apart from his wife's scolding he does not seem to have suffered, as did Clare, from the stigma of eccentricity. Not many years elapsed before "a Young Gentleman of Oxford," hearing reports of a poetical thresher, asked Stephen to write him a letter in verse. The result, the first of Duck's recorded poems, was of such a quality, and so unexpectedly free from rusticity, that it was considered not to have been his own composition. Although the young gentleman of Oxford did not pursue the matter, the poem fell into the hands of some clergymen in the neighbourhood, who, finding it to be meritorious, visited Duck and encouraged him to continue writing.

Henceforward Duck's fame spread, first amongst the notables of the district, and eventually to Court and to the Queen. In a few months his name became a household word. The curious and rich visited him at Charlton, giving him presents and promises and subjects on which he should write. In 1730 Queen Caroline herself received him at Windsor, and settled on him an annuity of £30 a year and a small house at Richmond.

Despite the adulation that was showered upon him, with its inevitable train of jealousy and intrigue, Duck "was not lifted up with the Character some People gave him, and talk'd of Fame absolutely like a Philosopher." His attitude towards his own poems (and in view of his character in other respects we may believe Spence in this) was modest and at the same time shrewd. "Gentlemen indeed, he said, might like 'em, because they were made by a poor Fellow in a Barn; but that he knew, as well as any body, that they were not really good in themselves."

Earlier in this chapter we have seen something of the growing prejudice in eighteenth century England against the breaking down of social barriers. On the part of the upper and middle classes this was largely occasioned by a reluctance to hear dissentient voices, which might challenge the order of their society built up under the renewed stability of the monarchy. When a figure such as Duck, amenable, respectful and flattering in his gratitude came to be transplanted from his native Wiltshire to mingle with the best society of the land, his mentors no longer questioned his right to such an elevation, but were immediately at pains to educate him to become an inconspicuous unit in his new social caste. As Duck had not solicited these changes, nor had struggled into this new society unaided, it was gratifying and philanthropic to assist him, and during the first years after his discovery he never lacked a patron.

From the letters of Dr. Alured Clarke, who undertook the task of supervising Duck's belated education, it is possible to understand more sympathetically why the thresher-poet, who might have brought the countryside into the salons of the Augustans, was metamorphosed into an Horatian coupleteer. Stephen, Dr. Clarke assures us, had a "great aversion to drollery, ridicule or jingle." There is certainly little evidence that Duck possessed a sense of humour, but although he tended by inclination towards religion, Dr. Clarke's literary diet seems austere and unimaginative. The works of Swift and Montaigne were to be denied to him, but he should read Burnet's *Theory of the Earth* and Ray's *Wisdom of God in the Creation*. He was to learn Latin, get Pope's *Essay on Criticism* by heart, and Dr. Clarke only allowed him to read Shakespeare in its entirety "being very well satisfied that Stephen will suck the flowers, and leave all the puns and low conceits behind him." It was a rigorous course in civilizing according to neo-classical tenets, and one from which neither the thresher nor the poet recovered.

The same year that Duck became a beneficiary of the Queen a pirated edition of his works appeared in London and enjoyed an immediate success, being reprinted nine times. The authoritative edition, under the title *Poems on Several Occasions*, was not published until six years later. However inaccurate the version, Duck was much read, and discussed in literary and court circles even more. It was scarcely surprising in view of the stir he had created that when Eusden, the Poet Laureate, a "drunken sot of a parson," died, Duck was mooted as a likely candidate for that office.

Grub Street had much to say and to speculate on the appointment, which fell in the end to Cibber. Amongst those who watched the outpourings of venom and partisanship were Pope, Gay, and Swift. Swift delivered a bitter *Quibbling Epigram* at Duck; possibly he was angered that the preferment he had been denied was within the reach of an upstart in the realm of letters. Pope's attitude was equivocal. As a near neighbour of Duck he knew him personally, and wrote that "he is a harmless man." But as a poet he seems to have despised him, and he is said (though without any very solid foundation) to have instigated much of the satire that was levelled against the "translated" thresher. Pope certainly cannot have been pleased to hear the unfavourable comparisons of his own work to Duck's, and it may be that he had recourse to the same expedient as a friend of Thomson, who, says Dr. Clarke, decried the thresher on all occasions, as he considered him to be a rival to the author of *The Seasons*.

Whereas to some critics Duck continued to be "the Admiration of the present Age," the mock encomium that appeared in *The Gentleman's Magazine* in 1735 under the signature of "Benjamin Drake, Yeoman," is typical of the heavy-handed wit that Stephen silently endured.

> Hail! Stephen Duck, with praise around begirt,
> Well hast thou waddl'd thro' the country dirt:
> With honest labour, and industrious care,
> Hard was thy task, to bring around the year.

It is said that Duck received such sallies as this with "the stolid composure of the class from which he had sprung." Whether this composure was more than skin-deep, or whether he suffered like Burns or Keats from such indiscriminate sniping, it is impossible to say. Whatever his feelings were, he never attempted to reply.

Despite the divided opinions on his poetic merits, the Queen continued to bestow her favours on the thresher-poet. In 1733 he was made a Yeoman of the Guard and married for the second time, his former wife having died three years previously, on the eve of his rise to fame. Two years later he was appointed librarian and general custodian of Queen Caroline's strangely-conceived fantasy, Merlin's Cave. William Kent, acting under the Queen's instructions, had built this hybrid pleasure-house in Richmond Park in a style that faltered between classic and romantic. A Palladian façade under a thatched roof greeted the visitor, while behind an ogee doorway Stephen Duck waited to perform his duties as guide to the interior. Merlin himself, together with his secretary, was modelled there in wax, and an ill-assorted company which included Queen Elizabeth and Minerva completed the tableau.

Perhaps it was to escape from his strange surroundings that led Duck that same year to undertake an excursion to the West Country, a description of which he recorded in verse. By a curious coincidence a tour over much the same area undertaken by Bloomfield some seventy years later proved an equally memorable experience, and was commemorated by the farmer's boy in his poem *The Banks of Wye*. One of the objects of Duck's excursion was to revisit his birthplace, Charlton, in order to be present at the first of a series of annual Threshers' Feasts, endowed in his honour by Lord Palmerston, and which continue to this day.

Sensing, perhaps, that his popularity would soon be on the wane, and because by now he had amassed a sizable collection of verses, Duck published his *Poems on Several Occasions* in 1736. The bulk of his work failed in any way to fulfil the promise of excellence contained in his earlier poems. The book enjoyed a considerable success, but to even his most loyal friends it was becoming increasingly apparent that the thresher was not progressing as a poet. One of these friends, probably Spence, tried to persuade Duck to give up writing before the results became too lamentable. In 1741 Stephen replied to his friend "Laelius," saying that he still had the "itch of Scribbling,' and pleading, quite reasonably,

> And shall I not indulge my harmless Pen,
> And have my Way, as well as other Men?

As much now as at the beginning of his career as a poet, Duck himself was not persuaded of the intrinsic merits of his Muse. This did not seem to have been merely diffidence, but a shrewd realization of the inevitable transience of his fame. "'Tis my Delight," he claimed, "My Pleasure, and my Happiness to write." He would not deny himself this pleasure to preserve an immortality that he did not believe would be his lot.

In 1737 Queen Caroline died; so, some years later, did Duck's second wife. In 1744 he married for the third time, and two years afterwards was considered sufficiently advanced in his study of the classics to be admitted to Holy Orders. The benevolent influence of the Queen continued after her death. He was appointed first as a regimental chaplain, and a year later as preacher in Kew Chapel. His presence in the pulpit is said to have drawn great crowds of the curious, but his congregations remained large even after the initial excitement had died down.

Earlier in his life Spence recorded that "his common Talk is made up of the good Stile, with a mixture of the Rustick." Probably not much rusticity remained in his preaching days; in little but the name was the thresher-poet linked with the land he sprang from. Doubtless he made a conscientious parish priest, but after his appointment as Rector of Byfleet in 1752 there is little left to record of his life. His stipend of £130 a year was reasonably generous; his life should have been easy and pleasant in his country retirement. But tranquillity was not granted him. Four years after he arrived at Byfleet he drowned himself in the Thames at Reading.

The character of Stephen Duck seems to have been sincere and ingenuous, though it is necessary to make allowances for a certain fulsomeness in the written accounts of his life, owing to the hagiographic tendencies of eighteenth-century promotors and preface-writers. A poet like Duck, who had a great capacity for friendship, who was deferential and a respecter of station, was far more likely to secure and retain the benefits of patronage than a man of, say, Savage's temperament. Duck's case is an example of patronage at its best. The thresher was secured from want, helped in the way that was (even if mistakenly) thought best for him, and never threatened by abandonment or insecurity until he was well established in his new vocation. It may be judged that the continued philanthropy of his patrons was not a little due to Duck's own engaging personality. For the good of his own poetry Stephen was altogether too amenable. Amongst his early poems only one, the lines *On Poverty*, was written to please himself. All the others were written at the suggestion of, or in gratitude to, some benefactor. It is little wonder, therefore, that the majority of Duck's poems have a singular lack of spontaneity and are written on a heterogeneous selection of subjects. Dr. Clarke, soon after Duck's first reception at Court, wanted him to be relieved of the burden of writing verses for anyone except the Queen. He already sensed that Stephen, always obliging and flatteringly grateful, would have little time to write as the spirit moved him. Miss Davis, who, apart from Mr. Blunden, is the only critic since Southey to investigate the small niche Duck occupies in the temple of literature, concludes that this self-suppression had a considerable influence on his personality.

Duck felt bound to please his patrons; indeed, this passion for showing gratitude seems to have made him willing to change not only his characteristic poetic style, but his very personality; and a certain emptiness of spirit must have come in middle age to a man who had denied himself the right to his own personality.

Emotionally Stephen was noticeable only for his intense feeling towards literature and music. In human relationships we can read caution and candid good sense into his words and deeds, and a complete freedom from passion or a desire to shine. He was a man of limited vision, and utterly lacking in imagination. In this he was fortunate as he never felt stirred to consider the state of the society into which he had been adopted, or to view with any realism the general conditions that prevailed in the society that he had left. His social conscience was never troubled, and his mind not given to speculation. If it had been the course of his preferment might not have been so smooth. That the serene myopia with which he wrote "contended Poverty's no dismal Thing" was not part of a double game he was playing with his patrons may be judged by the unwavering constancy of this *leitmotif*, from the poems before patronage began to his last productions. There was no fiery soul lodged in Duck's breast, and one is tempted to believe that, at least after the first poetic blaze was dimmed, Stephen preferred to write occasional verse as it afforded a better opportunity to practise the mechanics of poetry without the trouble of inspiration or thought.

> Who can be silent, when they view
> This fair Creation, wrought by *You*?

enquired the erstwhile thresher, on seeing *A Screen, work'd in Flowers by Her Royal Highness Anne, Princess of Orange*. Obviously Stephen himself could not. It was Duck's greatest weakness (and it is inherent in the malleability of his character) that he could not fix his eye firmly on his subject—the only subject on which he was qualified to write—the land.

It is the men who have been least dependent on their fellow-creatures who have been the best interpreters of nature. The circumstances of Duck's life were too closely interrelated to human affairs to allow him to unify the vision and the voice of the countryman. Duck and Bloomfield were diverted into the ways of cities and men, Clare retained the independence of the peasant, and so, in the isolation of their country vicarages, did those two clergymen, Relph and Barnes, who made poetry from the simplicity of their lives.

In studying the poetry of a man such as Duck, whose work was never inspired and was sometimes bad, but which nevertheless possessed, at least in one poem, a distinct and individual charm, it is difficult to fix one's standards of judgment. Mr. Blunden is convinced that special critical standards must be created for peasant-poets writing on peasant themes.

A man writing of the poultry-yard or of threshing or the rules of the weather must be judged according to his humanity, experience, sense of proportion, power of phrase, what you will—but not by the immediate reference to great dramatists, novelists, philosophic stylists.

Even if this is special pleading before the bar of literary merit, it does not excuse the majority of Duck's works from a critical appraisal on terms of equality with all his contemporaries. Duck chose to write on themes common to the general writer, and not exclusively within the province of the peasant-poet. For the purposes of criticism he could not claim the benefits of being a thresher-poet for any of his verses except *The Thresher's Labour*. On all other occasions the biographical aspect is irrelevant to criticism. If he chose not to play on the home pitch we cannot mitigate his defeat by pleading the difficulty of the ground. These same considerations will be seen to apply equally to Robert Bloomfield, whose poetic merit was negligible after he had described the cycle of his life as a farmer's boy. In both these poets a lack of imagination limited their achievements. Once the factual record of their vocation had been described, the subject was considered to have been covered. Clare and Burns found an unending diversity of mood and vision unsuspected by the cyclical poets of the farming year.

Lest this seem too harsh a critical standard for a poet whose pretensions were small and whose achievements were not inconsiderable, it is best that Duck's poems should defend themselves. *The Thresher's Labour*, written early in Duck's career at the request of Mr. Stanley, is undoubtedly the work by which he should be remembered. It describes, as its title implies, the yearly round of a tasker such as Stephen himself; a man who for many centuries had been an unchanging, integral part of the English agricultural community.

The winter season, after the harvest has been gathered in, is the time Duck chooses to begin "to sing the Toils of each revolving Year." The threshing-floor has been prepared (an aspect of farm life that labourers nowadays are happily spared), and the farmer, a surly taskmaster, is talking to his men.

> So dry the Corn was carry'd from the Field,
> So easily 'twill thresh, so well 'twill yield;
> Sure large Days-works I well may hope for now:
> Come, strip, and try; let's see what you can do.

Soon Stephen and his companions are hard at work, whirling and striking their crab-tree staves in rhythm. Hand-threshing is obviously a physically arduous task.

> In briny Streams our Sweat descends apace,
> Drops from our Locks, or trickles down our Face.
> No Intermission in our Work we know;
> The noisy Threshal must for ever go.
> Their Master absent, others safely play;
> The sleeping Threshal does itself betray.

Compared to their noisy, seemingly endless task the leisure and tranquillity of a shepherd's life seem enviable to them. But the worst is not yet. When the corn is finished there comes an added discomfort.

> When sooty Pease we thresh, you scarce can know
> Our native Colour, as from Work we go:
> The Sweat, the Dust, and suffocating Smoak,
> Make us so much like *Ethiopians* look,
> We scare our Wives, when Ev'ning brings us home;
> And frighted Infants think the Bugbear come.
> Week after Week, we this dull Task pursue,
> Unless when winn'wing Days produce a new:
> A new, indeed, but frequently a worse!
> The Threshal yields but to the Master's Curse.
> He counts the Bushels, counts how much a Day;
> Then swears we've idled half our Time away:
> "Why, look ye, Rogues, d'ye think that this will do?
> Your Neighbours thresh as much again as you."

It is difficult to reconcile the picture of the tyrannical master in these lines with "kind MENALCAS, Partner of my Soul," who is revisited by Duck during his tour of the West Country, and is noted as being "A Farmer, once the Author's Master, and still his Friend." Perhaps the five-year interval had smoothed out the harsh memories of his labouring life.

These winter occupations over, the prospect of summer hay-making seems delightful, and the first few hours in the fields are sportive and gay. But the heat of the sun and the exertion of hard work exhausts them. Soon they seek the shade of a tree and the refreshment of scrip and beer, but

> Down our parch'd Throats we scarce the Bread can get;
> And, quite o'erspent with Toil, but faintly eat.
> Nor can the Bottle only answer all;
> The Bottle and the Beer are both too small.

The remainder of the day moves wearily to its close, and the labourers return home exhausted. In just such a condition Duck himself must have returned to his arithmetic books. The day-labourer gets little respite; next day he is back in the hayfields again, aided by a "Throng of prattling Females," who turn the hay. Duck obviously disapproves of this invasion, and in one of his occasional lengthy and studied similes (a classical technique learnt from Milton) he compares the women running for shelter during a sudden shower to a flock of sparrows.

> Thus have I seen, on a bright Summer's Day,
> On some green Brake, a Flock of Sparrows play;
> From Twig to Twig, from Bush to Bush they fly;
> And with continu'd Chirping fill the Sky:
> But, on a sudden, if a Storm appears,
> Their chirping Noise no longer dins your Ears:
> They fly for Shelter to the thickest Bush;
> There silent sit, and All at once is hush.

In descriptions such as this, and in moments of unfeigned enthusiasm (such as the thresher's immediate reaction to the untouched beauty of the ripe cornfield, "How beauteous all Things in the Morn appear,") the freshness and receptiveness of Duck's perception brings a rare touch of nature to a predominately urban half-century. If his vision had always been as sensitive as it was accurate, or as full of wonder and innocence as it was of precedents and classical conceits, Duck might have found Mossgiel or Helpstone in Wiltshire a century before their time.

If we are to believe Spence all the emotions and passions that we miss so much in Duck's poems were present in the man. Music stirred him to melancholy and delight, and when *Julius Caesar* was read to him, "he trembled as I read the Ghost's Speech . . . As I was reading to him, I observ'd that his Countenance chang'd often in the most moving Parts: His Eye was quick and busy all the time . . . I never saw Applause, or the shifting of proper Passions, appear so strongly in any Face as in his." These are surely the reactions of a more sensitive man than might be suspected from reading even the best of Duck's poetry. In his irregular ode, *To Death*, Stephen describes his own verses as "sedately dull," and from the accuracy of this self-criticism it is possible to guess that Duck was always in the unhappy position of being only semi-articulate. He could not express the feelings of his heart in the only ways that were known to him. His was the objective expression of a poet who, at least on occasions, was capable of being stirred subjectively.

After hay-making has been completed it is not long before the farmer summons his men to the harvest. Armed with their scythes they are in the fields at sunrise and, not without regret at disturbing so lovely a prospect, start to reap the crop.

> Behind our Master waits; and if he spies
> One charitable Ear, he grudging cries,
> "Ye scatter half your Wages o'er the Land."
> Then scrapes the Stubble with his greedy Hand.

When at last the corn has been reaped, and the harvest garnered, "Menalcas" is better pleased; but his irate accusations have a ring of authenticity about them, whereas Thomson's farmer, in the same circumstances, is more an ideal than an actual landowner.

> Behind the master walks, builds up the shocks,
> And conscious, glancing oft on every side
> His sated eye, feels his heart heave with joy.

As the two poems were virtually contemporaneous, the differences between the Arcadia with verisimilitude of Thomson, and Duck's unimaginative statements of fact make a most interesting comparison. To Thomson the harvest presented a scene of harmony, pleasure and accord.

> Before the ripened field the reapers stand
> In fair array, each by the lass he loves.

Duck knew well that "the tattling Croud" had no place amongst Wiltshire harvesters. Being close to the event Stephen did not hear so distinctly as Thomson.

> the blended voice
> Of happy labour, love, and social glee;

he could not detach himself and view his occupation as a landscape with figures. He knew the exhaustion and boredom of Arcady too well to be convinced that the happiest of men "drinks the pure pleasures of the rural life." Duck was realistic about his labours rather than discontented with them.

After the last load has been safely brought home, the surly task-master of the fields relaxes, and invites all the labourers to the traditional feast of harvest-home. This annual ceremony has never escaped the notice of the poets of the countryside. Tusser records that he gave his men "good cheer in the hall all harvest time long," and presented each ploughman with a goose. Thomson, and later Bloomfield, describe the celebrations, and only in the last century did the custom pass into desuetude. To Duck and his companions it was a time of great satisfaction and enjoyment. "Jugs of humming Ale" were generously plied, and momentarily the year's labour was forgotten.

> But the next Morning soon reveals the Cheat,
> When the same Toils we must again repeat;
> To the same Barns must back again return,
> To labour there for Room for next Year's Corn.

The same depressing thought occurred to Thomson:

> Thus they rejoice, nor think
> That with tomorrow's sun their annual toil
> Begins again the never-ceasing round.

Harvest-home brings the year full circle, simply and less circumstantially than in either Thomson's or Bloomfield's poems. Duck's cycle consists, in fact, of only three operations: threshing, hay-making and reaping. In scheme and execution the poem is sturdy and largely unembellished, though the poet has an unfortunate tendency to use classical similes and stilted language. End-stopped couplets were a tyrannous, but inevitable, form for a poet of Duck's generation to adopt. On the whole he uses them unobtrusively; but as he himself admitted when he recast *The Shunammite* out of its original Miltonic blank verse, they disguised his defects of sublimity, and allowed him to shelter his weakness of expression behind the rigid framework of the verse. *The Thresher's Labour* is, nevertheless, as Southey realized, "the best specimen of Stephen Duck's productions in verse." Had he continued in this vein his achievements might have been considerable. He himself acknowledged in *A Poem on Her Majesty's Birthday* that "My humble Muse can humble Subjects treat," but he never returned to the fields from which he had been transplanted. Instead of becoming more fluent in his interpretations of the natural surroundings he knew so well, he ceased to develop as a poet either technically or in inspiration. Within five years of his first reception by the Queen he had become as uncountrified as Shenstone's young squire who could breathe nowhere but in town. No longer were the woodlands a part of Duck's background, he was instead "Pleas'd with the silent Horror of the Grove." The Augustan desire to make order out of the chaos of nature, to regularize and formalize their landscapes, met with his entire approval. The natural landscape in which he had grown up was now crude and hostile,

> Till CHANDOS bad the dreary Desert smile
> With verdant Groves, and beautify'd the Soil.

The thresher had quickly learnt his lessons and become a child of the times.

The majority of Duck's verses do not merit a detailed study, but it is worth remarking on certain aspects of his writing. If one had to chose from the body of Duck's works the theme with which he was most concerned, it would be nothing so specific as the true picture of the labourer, or the state of husbandry. Duck tended to avoid the concrete and play with abstractions. Again and again throughout his poems we find the thresher moralizing on the evils resulting from avarice, and the right use of riches or poverty. Despite his high-minded censoriousness and his frequent declarations that money was a commodity far from his thoughts, one suspects that his life had been too closely connected with financial anxieties for them to have been without influence on him. But once again Duck chased the moral idea rather than the physical reality. In claiming that poverty could only frighten little souls, and comparing its terror to childish fears at night, he was doing his cause an injustice. Dr. Johnson was not alone in knowing that "slow rises worth by poverty depress'd." Duck is equally unconvincing when he declares that the poor enjoy their food more than the cloyed and care-worn rich. It might have been good policy to bolster the social conscience of the moneyed class in this way but it did not improve his poetry.

A second distinctive feature of Duck's collected verse is the extraordinary amount of gratitude he expressed, and flattery he delivered. This trait is doubtless commendable, but it would seem that Duck was haunted by his obligations to those who had assisted him in his rise to fame. In his zeal he was often denegrating and sometimes obsequious. In his pastoral, *Gratitude*, Duck realized that if Queen Caroline were "to patronize a Shepherd meanly born," "sometimes a Song, perhaps, she may require." Unhappily such effusions stifled the slender output of poems from his own experience.

Apart from *The Thresher's Labour* Duck does not often refer to his early occupation, and in only two other poems is it possible to catch a glimpse of the peasant united with the poet. In his earliest recorded poem, *To a Gentleman who requested a Copy of Verses from the Author*, Stephen explains why, because an "illit'rate Poet guides the Pen," he does not chose a lofty subject for his muse. If he were able, he claims, he would compose a Christiad. At this time the influence of Milton was strong upon him. Later, when he was more qualified to attempt an epic, had he so desired, the subject is never mentioned, and the precision of Pope rather than the grandeur of Milton encompassed his ambition. When he wrote his verse epistle to the gentleman from Oxford, however, he was acutely conscious of his limitations. But he was aware of the futility of pipe-dreams, and dismisses them, and his correspondent, with a reminder of the realities that should engross him.

> But why stand I my Fate accusing so?
> The Field calls me to Labour, I must go:
> The Kine low after Meat; the hungry Steed,
> Neighing, complains he wants his usual Feed.
> Then, Sir, adieu.

The last time that the voice of the peasant-poet is heard in Duck, and then fitfully, is some six years later in *A Description of a Journey to Marlborough, Bath, Portsmouth etc.* The sight of mowers at work near his native fields proves too much for him.

So with Ambition burns my daring Breast;
I snatch the Scythe, and with the Swains contest;
Behind 'em close, I rush the sweeping Steel;
The vanquish'd Mowers soon confess my Skill.

It is the houses of the rich, not the cottages of the poor, that Duck
visits on his tour, and the works of man that please him most. On
Salisbury Plain he pauses to consider sadly how the land might be
sweet with the Arcadian music of shepherds. But the shepherds he thinks
he sees are not men inspired as he was, but less fortunate in their
advancement; he saw them as Pope imagined them, not to be described "as shepherds at this day really are, but as they may be conceived
then to have been, when the best of men followed the employment."
It is not surprising, therefore, that on Salisbury Plain Duck found to his
regret that

> to his Mouth, the Shepherd ne'er applies
> His mellow Pipe, nor vocal Music tries:
> Propt on his Staff, he indolently stands;
> His Hands support his Head, his Staff his Hands;
> Or, idly basking in the sunny Ray,
> Supinely lazy, loiters Life away.

Stephen failed to apprehend the cogent reality of this situation, and
although Crabbe, towards the end of the century, credited Duck with
some consciousness of his position, it would seem that the thresher
never realized that he could, as a poet, be in any way different from
other poets, or be the forerunner of a tradition of rural singers. In
part Crabbe's bitter lines in *The Village* had been anticipated by Duck.
It was he who first challenged belief in the inherent joy and dignity
of labour; but he never formulated his thoughts, and often, as with
the shepherds of Salisbury Plain, he accepted a ready-made conception
alien to his natural belief, but which fell with less argument into the
mould that was prepared for it.

No poet can be attacked for lack of genius: it is a quality inbred
only in the great artist. In Duck's day it would have required an
intellectually stronger figure than he to voyage through those strange,
progenitive seas of thought alone. He must not be condemned for

what he did not do, but commended for rising, as few men before him had risen, from plough to pen.

> Save honest Duck, what son of verse could share
> The poet's rapture, and the peasant's care?
> Or the great labours of the field degrade,
> With the new peril of a poorer trade?

Crabbe was right to remind us of the courage and achievements of Duck rather than his shortcomings. No one was more conscious of these than the thresher himself, who, during the annual dinner given in his honour, wondered what immortality might be granted him. He realized sooner than many of his contemporaries that his fame was likely to be emphemeral, but consoled himself with the shrewd prophesy,

> Thus shall Tradition keep my Fame alive;
> The *Bard* may die, the *Thresher* still survive.

Day Trips to Parnassus

Horace Walpole, writing to Hannah More in 1784 about her discovery of the poetical milkwoman, Ann Yearsley, reminded his enthusiastic correspondent that

when the late Queen patronised Stephen Duck, who was only a wonder at first, and had not genius enough to support the character he had promised, twenty artisans and labourers turned poets, and starved. Your poetess can scarce be more miserable than she is, and even the reputation of being an authoress may procure her customers.

Walpole's recollection may serve as sufficient excuse for indulging in a brief reconnaissance into the ranks of uneducated poetasters who, either independently, or stimulated by Duck's success, tried their fortunes in print. The productions of such humble writers, inspired more by ambition than by skill, were, at least in the eighteenth century, of exceedingly little merit. But against the average standard of writers of this class one can judge more appreciatively the relative stature of those peasant-poets with whom this book is chiefly concerned.

The genius that inspired Burns and Clare, or the talent that made Duck and Bloomfield noticeable amongst their contemporaries, is wholly lacking in the verses that follow. Woodhouse, Bryant, Tatersal and Falconer represent the standards of the ordinary man with a will to write. Not only do they act as a foil to judgment of greater figures, they show the enormous enthusiasm and aspiration of the lowest, as well as the highest, orders of society in the pursuit of letters.

The education that had been considered so superfluous by writers on social problems from Mandeville to Cobbett, was earnestly desired and sought out by a far larger proportion of artisans and labourers than has been generally recognized. Not only have we the proof of this in their published works—a more feasible proposition for them since the inception of provincial printing presses—but in the reports of such observant travellers as the young German student, Carl Philipp Moritz. During his walking tour through England in 1782 he was frequently impressed by the high cultural level of working-class people. In Derbyshire he met a saddler who discoursed with him on Homer, Horace, and Virgil; and while lodging in London he remarked,

> My landlady, who is only a taylor's widow, reads her Milton; and tells me, that her late husband first fell in love with her, on this very account; because she read Milton with such proper emphasis. This single instance perhaps would prove but little; but I have conversed with several people of the lower class, who all knew their national authors, and who all have read many, if not all of them.

Such a testimony reflects some credit on the achievements of Charity School education, but it indicates still more an enthusiasm after learning that might be thought to have died down after the Renaissance.

The cheap price of books, and the quick sale of classical authors that Moritz observed, tended to increase the opportunities for ill-educated men to improve themselves. Earlier in the century it is possible to infer from Defoe's *Tour Through Great Britain* that in country districts the Tunbelly Clumsys were giving place to a squirearchy more inclined to letters than before, and this change did not fail gradually to influence the peasants themselves. The increasing artisan population of the towns was inevitably forced into a physical, if not spiritual, proximity to the world of books, and although conditions of labour were no less severe, and the hardships of living and working were no less acute, an increasing number of working men and women found solace in verse.

The artisan was never recognized as an unconscious heir of poetry. No bucolic tradition supported him, and for the most part his attempts in verse were grudgingly received by the eighteenth-century public. "Certain journeymen taylors, shoemakers, barbers, Spitalfield weavers," declared *The Monthly Review* in February 1778, "have presumed to make rhymes and discharge them on the Public." But it took more than the disapproval of the reviews to damp the ardour of such men. Poetry, as Richard West observed, had become "as universally contagious as the smallpox."

Writing in verse was a more natural method of expressing one's thoughts on any subject than it is today. The newly-created proletariat of the city, together with the peasants grounded only in the oral tradition of literature, were beginning to emerge as permanent and potentially sophisticated groups, with an unformed literary future. They did not, at this early period of the eighteenth century, spring forth fully armed with a peasant or artisan tradition in poetry. Regrettably they never fashioned the ballad and the folk-tale into a distinctive written form: working into a universal framework those qualities of sincerity and simplicity that the romanticists would hold to be the archetypes of poetic composition. They chose instead to follow the already exploited paths of sentimental moralism and neo-classical propriety. Against such competition the almost unlettered, instinctive poet was at an immediate disadvantage. He would be gauche at delicately-chiselled niceties, and laborious in his didacticism. It was not until Burns discovered the "kindely stede" of peasant-poets, and rooted them firmly to the land, that these incipient geniuses could establish the precedent to be anything but poor relations in poetic inspiration.

Almost inevitably the uneducated poet had to write from his own experience—in a sense autobiographically—in order to write well. Imagination, which is conditioned by a breadth of experience, is seldom very pronounced in a man whose vision is narrowed by his occupation and training. The peasant was a recorder more than an interpreter of nature; he was more at ease with specific descriptions than with general surveys. The growth of this peasant spirit, of observing the minutiae of nature rather than an unlocalized prospect from Cooper's or Grongar Hill, is to be seen in the slowly narrowing focus of all eighteenth-century nature poetry, culminating in the intense localism of Wordsworth and Scott. It would be rash to assume that the peasant-poet in any way influenced this change: the Romanticists, by fusing imagination to perception, disclosed a prospect for poetry at which no uneducated poet (unless Blake be included) had hinted.

But throughout the century the constant recurrence of untutored poets did not pass unnoticed. The public became increasingly interested in hearing the messages of children of nature, whether in the form of thresher, Gaelic hero or Tahitan savage.

> Pity the sandal'd swain, the shepherd's boy;
> He sighs to brighten a neglected name;
> Foe to the dull appulse of vulgar joy,
> He mourns his lot; he wishes, merits fame.

Shenstone, who himself helped James Woodhouse, the poetical cobbler, was only one of those who looked sympathetically to the land, that had already yielded up Duck, and where, perhaps, the rural ditties might not yet be mute.

One of the first of those who avowedly imitated Stephen Duck, in the hope of also copying that poet's rise to prosperity, was a weaver from Spitalfields, who published a miscellany of poems in 1731. *The Grub Street Journal* affected great concern at the possibility of a mass abandonment of loom and land. "The poor weaver," it asserted, "has been tempted to neglect his business, by Stephen Duck's good fortune, as he himself plainly tells us in the introduction to his *Miscellany* . . . . The best way to encourage the weaver would be . . . to wear the manufactures of Great Britain; and the most suitable encouragement to the thresher would be to give him a small farm in the country; laying both under an absolute restraint never more to write a line of verse." However ideal this treatment might have been, it was never carried out; and in the second half of the century Johnson had taken up the mantle of *The Grub Street Journal* in speaking of Woodhouse. "They had better furnish the man with good implements for his trade than raise subscriptions for his poems. He may make an excellent shoemaker, but can never make a good poet."

A year after the Spitalfields weaver had been laughed at and forgotten, Robert Dodsley, stocking-weaver, bookseller, and "gentleman usher to the Muses," published *The Muse in Livery*. Dodsley possessed a talent—and not exclusively a poetic one—that would have forced its way through any society. He had an Elizabethan flair for living, and the poems of Dodsley the footman, as he then was, would have come to print regardless of the example of Stephen Duck. But he knew of the thresher-poet, and watched his rise to favour. In an *Epitaph to Stephen Duck, on his first coming to Court*, he applauded Duck's integrity, and compared their early efforts to those of fledglings learning to fly on the foothills of Parnassus.

While Dodsley greeted a fellow-spirit in a different walk of life, many writers used Duck's name in their works in order to solicit help, express envy, or increase their own sales. John Frizzle, an Irish miller, who wrote some verses to Duck, published in *The Gentleman's Magazine*, voices the most common complaint.

> Were I a while from noise and dust released,
> ... ev'n I
> As well as you my little Skill might try.

Robert Tatersal, "a poor Country Bricklayer of Kingston upon Thames," was such another. On the title-page of his book, *The Bricklayer's Miscellany*, he pertinently demands

> Since Rustick Threshers entertain the Muse,
> Why may not Bricklayers too their Subjects chuse?

Poetry to him, one feels, was not the divine gift of God, rarely bestowed, but purely a means to an end. Stephen Duck, for four years the beneficiary of the Queen, was to provide the key with which he could unlock the door of his prison.

> And can you see, and pity not my Case?
> With Noise and Dust in this unhappy Place?
> Had I Access, and cou'd the *Trowel* leave,
> To Royal *Richmond* wou'd I come, believe.

Duck can hardly have relished the prospect, more especially as Tatersal is at pains to dwell on the improvement in the thresher's material prosperity rather than the merits of his poetry.

> O *Stephen, Stephen!* can you silent be?
> Or cease to sing her grateful Clemency?
> Who brought thee from the Field to better Cheer,
> Enlarg'd thy Bottle, and enrich'd thy Beer.

Tatersal's approach is that of a cynical and unsuccessful racketeer, pleading with Duck to be allowed to share the bounty that his credulous public had bestowed upon him. To qualify for such favours the brick-layer describes his own occupation in verse, always with an eye to the patronage he desired.

> Think on my Case admidst the horrid Din
> Of Swearing, Chawing, and of drinking Gin,

he pleads. *The Bricklayer's Labours* is closely modelled on Duck's poem, but, unlike its original, it is of little interest to even the most eclectic student of literature. As a study in the squalid, gin-soaked life of the working man, it has an appalling social significance.

The last poem in the *Miscellany*, *The Author's Wish*, is not with-out pathos. It describes the pipe-dreams of a man thoroughly dis-contented with his lot in life, but incapable of changing it for the better. The "secret Sparks above a common Ray" that he claimed to possess were of no use to him and brought him no happiness. Not often did such sparks blaze up with the tinder of preferment. But the existence of the aspiring bricklayer stands as a challenge to Mandeville's commonly-held opinion that "there is not a more contented People among us, than those who work the hardest and are the least Acquainted with the Pomp and Delicacies of the World."

The freedom from cant and custom that should have left the mind of Tatersal receptive to the slightest breath of original inspiration, gave him instead an insurmountable inferiority complex. Like so many poets who were denied by their birth many of the advantages that more fortunate men possessed, he confused the mental with the social hierarchy, and spent his life striving to imitate those whom his natural talents might have led him to excel.

The vogue for directly imitating Duck was short-lived. The last to use the thresher's name to help promote her own was Mary Collier, a laundress, who in 1739 published *The Woman's Labour*. Her thirty-two-page pamphlet neither has, nor claims, literary merit. "Tho' She pretends not to the Genius of Mr. DUCK, nor hopes to be taken Notice of by the Great, yet her Friends are of Opinion that the Novelty of a *Washer-Woman's* turning Poetess, will procure her some Readers," she declares in her preface. Public interest did not rise to the bait, and Mary Collier can have benefited little from her excursion into verse.

The ostensible excuse for her poem was the slighting reference Duck made in *The Thresher's Labour* to the work of women at haymaking. She immediately takes Stephen to task.

> So many Hardships daily we go through,
> I boldly say, the like *you* never knew.

Not only had she been a washerwoman; Mary claimed she had worked in the fields too, and she proceeds to give a very convincing picture of the burden of toil that was demanded of a working-class woman in the eighteenth century, with the small rewards she gained from it. Mary Collier was an outspoken woman, and not content with carrying the day in her dispute with Duck, she adds a plea for the rights of women that would delight any feminist.

> No Learning ever was bestow'd on me;
> My Life was always spent in Drudgery;
> And not alone; alas! with Grief I find,
> It is the Portion of poor Woman-kind.

The days of her own labour were now over, she claimed. She had ceased to char all day for sixpence, and "now I have retired to a Garret (the Poor Poet's Fate) . . . where I am endeavouring to pass the Relict of my days in Piety, Purity, Peace, and an Old Maid."

The avowed imitators of Duck were not the only, nor the most important of the proletarian poets of the eighteenth century. James Woodhouse, whose long life ranged between the early publications of Duck and Clare, is one of the few examples of a peasant-poet who remained unspoilt and died happily. His copious verse is long forgotten, and such remembrance as he has is for occasioning Dr. Johnson's advice, "give nights and days, Sir, to the study of Addison." Although Johnson dismissed the general interest in the poetical yeoman as "all vanity and childishness," he was himself most curious to see him, and through meeting Woodhouse he met also Mrs. Thrale.

In 1743, at the age of eight, Woodhouse left school. For many years he lived quietly and unambitiously as a cobbler and yeoman farmer at Rowley, on the outskirts of Birmingham, with an inclination towards letters that never interfered with his work. Shenstone, whose estate, The Lessowes, lay nearby, discovered his poetic talent and assisted him in various ways. By being allowed the use of his library Woodhouse was able to continue his education, and when Shenstone planned the landscaping of his grounds Woodhouse assisted him in the project. Woodhouse was proud of his patron and loved The Lessowes as dearly as its owner. Most of the poems in his first volume, which was published in 1764, are copious expansions of such themes.

> near my feet, by tasteful SHENSTONE led,
> A limpid lake dissects the verdant mead
> With scollop'd sides, that now, with peaceful breast,
> Receives the image of the skies imprest;
> While silver-fringed vapours glide below,
> And mimic suns in neither regions glow:
> Now breathes a ruffling zephyr o'er the glades,
> And ev'ry fair celestial object fades;
> But soon again subsides the tranquil stream,
> And o'er its bosom brighter glories gleam.

Woodhouse interlaced his rambling descriptive passages with pontifically correct moral sentiments, and his judgments on life and literature are all grounded on similar standards. Thomson, for instance

> sung the seasons of the circling year;
> But not a mere description to rehearse,
> He crown'd each pregnant scene with moral verse.

Subsequent compositions, including the long verse-novel, *The Life and Lucubrations of Crispinus Scriblerus*, did nothing to enhance or detract from the inoffensive monotony of Woodhouse's achievements. In his later years, after the death of Shenstone, he owned a small bookshop in London, which kept him from poverty until his death in 1820 at the age of eighty-five.

Southey is more hopeful than accurate in detecting an evolutionary process in Woodhouse's verse. It would have been helpful to his thesis if there had been. But neither with Duck, nor with Woodhouse, was there an inevitable decline in merit after their wild Muses had been tamed. Except for *The Thresher's Labour* both poets have an evenness of expression that indicates a mechanical, not an inspirational, method of composition, and shows how astonishingly faithful both poets were to their original concepts of poetry-making. Southey argues as an apologist for the countryside that had failed to produce an uncorrupted, negatively-capable, poet.

A process, indeed, is observable, both in the verses of Woodhouse and Stephen Duck, which might be looked for, as almost inevitable: they began by expressing their own thoughts and feelings, in their own language; all which, owing to their stations in life, had a certain charm of freshness as well as truth; but that attraction passes away when they begin to form their style upon some approved model, and they then produce just such verses as any person, with a metrical ear, may be taught to make by a receipt.

Negative capability, that state defined by Keats as "being in uncertainties, mysteries, doubts, without any irritable reaching after fact and reason," is, perhaps, more essential to an uneducated than to an intellectually mature poet. Keats regretted those half-truths that Coleridge could not leave in their beauty, but hounded down and exposed out of intellectual curiosity. How much more should we regret the inability of all peasant-poets except Burns and Clare to suggest instead of to define, to be engulfed in, rather than detached from, their subject. The eighteenth-century writer possessed little or no capacity—or desire—to associate himself with the sparrow pecking in the gravel, and with the grain at which it pecked; but nature demands such a denial of self from her truest interpreters. It is the passive quality of subjective being that brings the third, life-giving dimension to the plane surface of objective description. Shakespeare, who possessed this quality to the full (as any great dramatist must), is intuitively a better and less laborious mirror of the seasons than Thomson, who devoted himself more exclusively to this task, but viewed their pageant without associating himself with it. Clock-a-Clay's pulse beats from Clare's heart, and reflects the unenquiring mystery of a cowslip-centred world. Thomson's insects, or Duck's, or Woodhouse's, or Bloomfield's after him, would be viewed, however sympathetically, through eyes that were not virginal because they had seen other things.

"The mediocres," wrote Southey, "have long been a numerous and an increasing race, and they must necessarily multiply with the progress of civilization." The second half of the eighteenth century produced more than enough uneducated poets to justify such a remark. Sometimes mediocrity was inherent in the man, as in the case of Henry Jones, who was brought from Ireland by the Earl of Chesterfield, quarrelled with his patron, failed to fulfil himself as a poet, and later had the misfortune to be run over when drunk. Sometimes a man, gifted in other spheres, unwisely strayed into verse. William Huntington, the tenth—and illegitimate—son of the wife of a Kentish labourer, had no aptitude for poetry, though he was undeniably gifted as a preacher of Methodism. Unfortunately he occasionally wrote doggerel that contrasts sadly with his virile and pungent prose. One of the most well-thought-of verse-writers of her day, the pathos of whose life-story overcame the indifference of her verse, was Ann Yearsley, a milkwoman of Bristol.

Lactilla (for so Ann Yearsley called herself) knew better than almost any poet the bitterness of poverty and starvation. She sold milk from door to door, mothered a rapidly-increasing family, but failed to prosper. When a Mr. Vaughan discovered her gift for poetry, she, her six children and her mother were dying from want; indeed the latter it proved impossible to save. These circumstances came to the ears of Hannah More, who immediately adopted Lactilla's cause as her own. She wrote to her numerous friends, Horace Walpole and Mrs. Montagu amongst them, lobbying on behalf of the unfortunate but talented milkwoman. "It is not intended," she assured them, "to place her in such a state of independence as might seduce her to devote her time to the idleness of Poetry." Ann was to be a wife and a mother first and foremost; but the most pressing reason for collecting subscriptions was to gain for her the wherewithal to live. "It is not fame, but bread, which I am anxious to secure to her."

Ann Yearsley was twenty-eight when Hannah More adopted her. She had had no formal education, beyond being taught to write by her brother. She knew nothing of grammar, and although she read intensely, her range was small. The melancholy of *Night Thoughts* and an inflated grandeur, imitated from *Paradise Lost*, show the two greatest influences on her writing. Of Dryden, Thomson, Spenser or Prior she had not even heard. A small volume of translations from the *Georgics* she greatly admired, and her knowledge of classical myth was gleaned from the pictures in print-shop windows.

In the first enthusiasm for her protégée Hannah More declared, as Spence did of Duck, that she had a natural critical faculty. "Without having ever conversed with any body above her own level, she seems to possess the general principles of sound taste and just thinking." The desire to find the natural poet, critically instinctive, and perfect in judgment, has already been commented on; Hannah More, a woman of unbounded enthusiasm, was certain that she had discovered such a "natural" milkmaid. Even Walpole, replying to Miss More in 1784, had few reservations. "Were I not persuaded by the samples you have sent me, Madam, that this woman has talents, I should not advise her encouraging her propensity, lest it should divert her from the care of her family, and, after the novelty is over, leave her worse than she was."

The indefatigable Hannah More secured a good subscription list, and Lactilla's poems were published in 1785. Society was charmed by the unacrimonious melancholy that they expressed, and the lurid, heavily-powerful use of descriptive words.

> The too gaudy Sun
> Shines not for me,

she complains in the opening poem, *Night*,

> no bed of Nature yields
> Her varied sweets; no music wakes the grove;
> No vallies blow, no waving grain uprears
> Its tender stalk to cheer my coming hour;
> But horrid Silence broods upon my soul,
> With wing deep-drench'd in Misery's torpid dews.

"I should be sorry to see the wild vigour of her rustic muse polished into elegance," Hannah More wrote to Mrs. Montagu. This was a new approach to a proletarian poet. Half a century after Duck had been dieted with a belated neo-classical education, Ann Yearsley was to be allowed to use her perfect ear and instinctive judgment as she pleased. Unfortunately such freedom came to the wrong person, and too late. The culture that she received would seem to have influenced her little, and grammatical correctness was the extent of her adult learning.

In her verses Lactilla expresses due humility and a desire to perfect her craft through the good offices of her new-found friends. In particular she asked them to

> Teach me to paint the tremors of the soul
> In Sorrow's deepest tints.

In the dedication of a subsequent volume she claimed that her works were "the effusions of NATURE only," but she freely admitted that nature needed to be perfected by the art of hands more skilled than her own. Thus she abandoned the freedom of expression that Hannah More had wished her to retain, and willingly disciplined herself as a novitiate to the established poetic order. Her orthodoxy can be seen in the lines she addressed *To Mrs. V-N.*

> Bright sentiment, if unimprov'd, must die,
> And great ideas, unassisted, fall;
> On Learning's wing we pierce th'empyreal sky;
> But Nature's untaught efforts are but small.

Typical of Ann Yearsley's early poems is *Clifton Hall,* which presents something of a discursive seasonal commentary on the countryside around Bristol with which she was familiar. Autobiographical material is sparse, except when, in the depths of winter,

> half sunk in snow,
> LACTILLA, shivering, tends her fav'rite cow.

But melancholy thoughts are never far distant. The sight of Clifton Church, where her mother lay buried, leads, as might be expected, to a lengthy and lugubrious meditation. Even the joyful advent of spring is accompanied by a seasonal warning to the village girls.

> Ye blooming maids, beware,
> Nor the lone thicket with a lover dare.
> No high romantic rules of honour bind
> The timid virgin of the rural kind;
> No conquest of the passions e'er was taught,
> No meed e'er given them for the vanquish'd thought.

Clifton Hall is a more sustained poem than Ann Yearsley commonly wrote, but like all her verses it contains many of the faults, and few of the virtues, of an uneducated poet's writings. Personification is common, imagery and metaphor florid and laboured. Her style was puffed out rather than elevated, and more affected than natural. Southey was puzzled by the slight results from so promising a potential when he summed up her work. "With extraordinary talents, strong feelings, and an ardent mind, she never produced a poem which found its way into any popular collection."

The sale of the first volume of her poems produced £350, which sum Miss More and Mrs. Montagu put in trust for Ann and administered on her behalf. It was not an entirely satisfactory arrangement. Patronage puts its recipient under an obvious debt of gratitude, but Lactilla's money was her own; and despite the obligation she felt towards Hannah More she considered herself entitled to some voice in the administration of the trust. Inevitably there was a quarrel, which reflected little credit on Hannah More. To be so much as questioned put that lady on her dignity, and made discussion impossible. "Are you *mad*, Mrs. Yearsley? or have you drank a glass too much?" she exclaimed when she was asked for a copy of the deed of trust. Further interviews produced no accord. Hannah referred to Lactilla as a savage, and accused her of a miscellany of failings, such as gambling, drunkenness, and extravagance. Ann defended herself fairly effectively, but they were never reconciled.

Without the business ability and influence of Hannah More, Ann Yearsley never prospered. Her books continued to sell for a few years, but interest waned, just as it had with her predecessors, and as Walpole had predicted it might with her. For a while she ran a circulating library near Bristol, grew penurious again, and died, probably insane, in 1806.

Apart from being (if we except Mary Collier) the only woman proletarian poet, there is little that can be satisfactorily said either in praise or in blame of Ann Yearsley. Her station in life was one of the least conducive to the production of verse that it is possible to imagine, and we can only judge her achievements sympathetically in the manner that Johnson judged a woman preaching. Her early reading in *Paradise*

Lost had an unfortunate effect upon her style, for Miltonic verse, as Keats realized, "cannot be written but in the vein of art"—and artlessness was essential to a writer with so meagre an intellectual equipment as Lactilla.

The wide dissemination of Milton's poems even amongst the lower classes of society, and the influence they had amongst poets who were not initially prejudiced in their favour, is one of the most interesting and constant factors conditioning the growth of the uneducated poet movement in England. Ann Yearsley seems to have received other influences too late for them to be very apparent. She never developed as a poetess, and perhaps her lack of response to cultural opportunities helped to turn Hannah More against her. But poetry could never be an all-absorbing occupation for her. She was not responsible just to herself, but to her family; and they surely must have echoed Crabbe's cry,

> Can poets soothe you, when you pine for bread?

A poet whose early years were spent in circumstances as miserable as those of Ann Yearsley was William Falconer. He was not a poet of the countryside, but he was quite uneducated; and some mention of him is not irrelevant if only because of his successful use of "terms of Art" in his major work, *The Shipwreck*. The loathness of Augustan poets to call a spade a spade is too well known to need reiterating. Dryden, in his preface to *Annus Mirabilis*, provided a loophole by strenuously defending the inclusion of technical and nautical words in that poem, "the terms of Art in every Tongue bearing more of the Idiom of it than any other words." Falconer, therefore, was never questioned when he wrote of robands, ear-rings, top-gallant-yards and rolling tackle, because the precedent had already been set, and the public were more inclined to learn about the phenomena of the sea than cavil at the particularity of their description. Instruction abounds in Falconer's poem, not only in his set passages of reflective didacticism, but in his accounts of such little-known matters as the breaking of a water-spout by gunfire, or the vivid changes of colour on the skin of a dying dolphin.

Falconer became a sailor by necessity at the age of twelve or thirteen. He was the son of an insolvent barber in Edinburgh, and both his brother and sister were deaf and dumb. Despite his strong love of nature and the land, which had it been indulged might have made him a sensitive peasant-poet, he was

> Forlorn of heart, and by severe decree,
> Condemned reluctant to the faithless sea.

An eighteenth-century sailor had less freedom, fewer opportunities for self-help, and more unattractive surroundings than any other class of man. The landsman at least had the seventh day at leisure, but the seaman might in many respects, as Johnson realized, as well have been in prison as on a ship.

> His labours cease not with declining day,
> But toils and perils mark his wat'ry way.

At the age of eighteen Falconer had succeeded so well in his occupation that he had become second mate of the *Britannia*, a vessel that was lost by shipwreck in the Mediterranean. He was one of the three survivors, and it is on this incident that his chief poem is based. Not until twelve years later, in 1762, did he write *The Shipwreck*; the poem was an immediate success. Memories of *Annus Mirabilis* were stirred, patriotism and sentiment were excited, and the fashionable world took Falconer to its heart.

> His verse no laurel wreath attempts to claim,
> Nor sculptured brass to tell the poet's name.
> If terms uncouth and jarring phrases wound
> The softer sense with inharmonious sound,
> Yet here let listening sympathy prevail,
> While conscious Truth unfolds her piteous tale!

Falconer's change of fortune allowed him to continue writing, under patronage, from the quarterdeck of *The Royal George*, for he had obtained a midshipman's commission in the Royal Navy. He found himself a "Miranda" to whom he addressed mannered verses, and rashly embarked on political and satirical rhymes which did nothing to improve his poetical reputation. Every few years he revised and enlarged *The Shipwreck*. In 1769, the year he published (as he was well fitted to do) a marine dictionary, Falconer's ship was wrecked on a passage to India, and all hands were lost.

Only in the sea did Falconer find strength as a poet; he wrote best about those things that he knew best. *The Shipwreck*, which uses the machinery of a sentimental love-story as the unifying theme throughout the poem, is consequently of very uneven quality. When the author is dealing with his seamen and his storms he writes from his own observation with great power and precision. But when the affairs of the romantic lovers, and digressions, ornaments and comparisons are added, the air of verisimilitude vanishes, and description is suspended in favour of banalities. It is, not unnaturally, to the shipwreck itself that one turns in order to appreciate Falconer's greatest powers. So accurately is the succession of orders and events recorded that it is a technical miracle that the couplets can move at all through the jumble of "terms of Art."

> "Reef top-sails, reef!" the master calls again.
> The halyards and top-bow-lines soon are gone,
> To clue-lines and reef-tackles next they run.

It cannot be called great poetry, but it is ingenious verse, and it holds the reader's attention: at times it is most stimulating. There is none of the panic or drunkenness of a Byronic shipwreck. Falconer was more concerned with formulating his own experience than giving rein to his imagination; in consequence it is a far more convincing, though less amusing, shipwreck than that which precipitated young Juan into the arms of Haidée.

Dryden was not ashamed to learn about life at sea: Byron would have scorned to admit ignorance. But Falconer knew, perhaps too well, the actions and reactions of sailors to the challenge of the elements. He was a peasant of the sea, with the same advantages and weaknesses as his land-locked brothers in verse. He felt obliged to express patriotism, unconsciously uttered platitudes, and was quite lacking in fancy or imagination. To his credit is a more than ordinary ability to describe with realism events from his own experience. In this he had an advantage over the ploughman-poet; all English poets have considered themselves sufficiently knowledgeable to write of country matters, but few have approached the ocean with the same confidence. Falconer was considered authoritative and original; his subject was new, and he did not need to have any sense of inferiority in approaching it. The opening scene of *The Tempest* is the nearest parallel in vivid reality to the storm in *The Shipwreck*, and the boatswain in Falconer's poem is blood-brother to the "whoreson, insolent noisemaker" of Shakespeare's creation when "like a hoarse mastiff through the storm he cries."

It would not be difficult to discover afresh many more poets, who on account of their birth or occupation would qualify to be included in this chapter. But already the boundaries have been stretched to incorporate uneducated poets from all walks of life, and the intention of this interlude is to be representative, not exhaustive, and to furnish a background of poetic endeavour, not an eighteenth-century *Stuffed Owl*. Only one further poet will be mentioned, James Frederick Bryant, the most part of whose poetry followed the oral and unsophisticated tradition of the ballads more than it simulated Augustan refinement.

Bryant's poems are what we might expect from a talented pipe-maker; they have no pretence at learning or book-knowledge, and they are written carelessly and chattily—often so that they could be sung to the accompaniment of his violin. His earliest verses, written to please the itinerant Irish labourers with whom he worked for a time at Woolwich, were composed in the manner of broadsides to celebrate local incidents and scandals.

> In Woolwich town does live a lass,
> I call her Wanton Betty,

begins one such jingle. These songs were written for just such people as Bryant was himself, and although there is little poetic merit in them they have a greater freedom of movement, rhythm and expression than poems written by the proletariat for the aristocracy. Nowadays, when it is frequent to decry writing down to one's public, it is salutary to learn from eighteenth-century unlettered poets that it is equally a fault to write up.

Patriotic songs were in great demand amongst Bryant's alehouse clientele, and the poet often earned himself food and drink by fitting new words to old tunes in the inn parlour. A stanza from *A Song on the "Princess Royal,"* designed to be sung to the tune *Of a noble Race was Shenkin*, gives an idea of his ability in this sphere.

> Then came a valiant Welchman,
>   Hur name was Tom Lewellyn;
> Says he, hur cannot rest nor sleep,
>   'Till the Yankees hur was killing.
> For since they'll not be rul'd
>   By us that did maintain her,
> We'll make them feel
> Our fire and steel,
>   And that's the way to gain her.
>   Fal de ral, etc., etc.

Bryant was born in 1753, the son of a clay-pipe maker in Bristol. A love of books and learning grew on him gradually and made him an unenthusiastic apprentice to his father's trade. Before long he deserted Bristol for London where he pursued a variety of occupations— bricklayer, hod-carrier and member of a press-gang. After marrying he returned home, where, his parents having died, he started to make pipes on his own. Whilst his wife tended the kiln, Bryant peddled his wares round the West Country. It was while he was waiting to be ferried back over the Severn and was trying to earn his passage-money by singing in the inn, that a gentleman, later to be his patron, dis- covered him.

Bryant never became a successful or a fashionable poet; only his working-class companions welcomed his singing. When, after his sight had begun to fail, he set himself up in a small book- and print-shop in London, he published his own poems together with his biography. But the sales do not seem to have been great. In 1787 there was little desire for poetry that possessed neither matter nor art. At the end of his volume he attempted to remedy the defect, and included two poems written in a more high-flown manner, full of hyperbole and derivative phrases ("the Morning, wrapt in mantle grey"), and in common with most peasant-poets, turgid with generalities and apos- trophe. At their best they have a heavy grandeur, as in *Morning*.

I sing a purple sky, with clouds of gold;
An orient horizon in a blaze
Of bursting glory, an enlighten'd earth
Of variegated form, and beauteous shades,
With all those overwhelming floods of light
That stream immediate from the fount of day.

But Bryant, though unconstrained, and nearer to the ideal of the unaffected, natural poet, never thought deeply or felt profoundly. He was an "idle singer of an empty day," more at ease with patter than poetry.

These men and women are representative of the uneducated writers of verse in the eighteenth century. The review does not disclose any hidden genius or even extraordinary talent. It does prove that the desire for poetic expression was widespread throughout all classes of society. In the eighteenth century more than at any other time in our history verse was an accepted medium for almost any sort of communication. But whereas the *gradus ad Parnassum* was temptingly easy, the hill was inviolate to all but the elect. The day-tripper will not stray off the beaten path, and without doing so he can never climb the mountain. These bricklayers, milkwomen and weavers, however, are not being arraigned for failure. The judgment is on ourselves for viewing such ephemeral and delicate originals through the harsh screen of two centuries. "Bad poetry—(if it be harmless in its intent and tendency)," wrote Southey, "can do no harm, unless it passes for good, becomes fashionable, and so tends to deprave still further a vitiated public taste, and still further to debase a corrupted language. Bad criticism is a much worse thing, because a much more injurious one, both to the self-satisfied writer and the assentient reader."

Robert Bloomfield

First made a Farmer's Boy, and then a snob,
A poet he became, and here lies Bob.
ROBERT BLOOMFIELD: MS. scribble, April 1823

In 1781 Robert Bloomfield, a fourteen-year-old farm boy, threw his old hat in the horse-pond, sold his smock for a shilling, and set off to London to turn shoemaker. It was not without regret that he left the East-Anglian farm where he had been employed for the past three years, but his employer, Mr. Austin, declared that he was too slightly built to be of much use on the land, and in consequence it had been decided to send him to London where he could join his two brothers, George and Nat, who were already established as journeymen shoe-makers in that city. "I am glad to find you are well and that you are willing to cum to London," wrote George. "Pack your Old Cloths up as clos as you can, don't waite, till Shoes or Shirts bee Mended. . . ." Robert took the stage-coach from Bury St. Edmunds and was met by his brother. He arrived "dressed just as he came from keeping sheep, hogs etc.—his shoes filled full of stumps in the heels. He, looking about him, slipt up—his nails were unused to a flat pavement. I remember viewing him as he scampered up:—how small he was."

There was little that would have attracted the attention of anyone outside his own family to the arrival in London of this young lad. He hated the city, but countrymen like himself were being drawn to the towns in increasing numbers at the turn of the century. Robert Bloomfield was seemingly destined to be absorbed by the

> Dependent, huge metropolis! where Art
> Her poring thousands stows in breathless rooms,
> Midst pois'nous smokes and steams, and rattling looms.

The countryside was far from him in his lodgings in Coleman Street, and for most youths the remembrance would quickly have been blurred and forgotten. His own thoughts, Robert recollected in a letter to his mother many years later, perpetually returned to the country around Honington, where he was born, and Sapiston, where he worked. His affection for Suffolk was never dimmed by city life, and he could always "see in imagination my old neighbours and things just as they were." The intensity and accuracy of Bloomfield's memories of Suffolk life, and the detachment with which he was able to record them as an anodyne to his tedious employment won him fame and admiration in his time. The emotions that he recollected in tranquillity were destined to be acclaimed when Wordsworth's were ignored.

Robert Bloomfield was one of six children, and his father, a tailor, had died when he was still an infant. In consequence there was little money that could be spared for Robert's education. His mother, who was the schoolmistress at Honington, taught him herself, and for a short while he went to the nearby village of Ixworth where he learnt to write a laborious copperplate but failed to learn, like the rest of his family, how to spell. After the unsuccessful attempt to make him a farmer it was decided, at his mother's request, that he should join his brothers in London; but even there he was of little real use. There were five men working in the garret with Robert, and the boy was employed on errands and odd jobs. It is from his brother George that we get a picture of the life he led during these first years in London.

We were all single men, lodgers at a shilling per week each, our beds were coarse, and all things far from being clean and snug, like what Robert had left at Sapiston. Robert was our man to fetch all things to hand. At noon he fetched our dinners from the cook's shop: and any one of our fellow-workmen that wanted to have anything fetched in, would send him, and assist in his work and teach him, for a recompense for his trouble.

Every day when the boy from the public-house came for the pewter pots, and to hear what porter was wanted, he always brought the yesterday's newspaper. The reading of the paper we had been used to take by turns; but after Robert came, he mostly read for us,—because his time was of least value.

He frequently met with words that he was unacquainted with: of this he often complained. I one day happened, at a book-stall, to see a small dictionary, which had been very ill used. I bought it for him for fourpence. By the help of this he in a little time could read and comprehend the long and beautiful speeches of Burke, Fox, or North.

Reading was more of a duty than a pleasure for him, but his interest was quickened by the review section of *The London Magazine* which contained a "Poet's Corner." He was stirred to emulation, and it was here that his first attempts at verse appeared. Making verses was an innocent pastime, and for some years he occasionally indulged in such compositions, encouraged by his sympathetic and watchful brother George. When his half-brother Isaac died at the age of sixteen George, who had gone home for the funeral, wrote to Robert asking him to compose an epitaph. "I have not braine Enough to make A Verse that will please my self," he admitted, "I think there is A Dificulty in A verse of this sorte for such A youth as Isaac, for he cannot be said to have any Charicter. . . ." Robert was not daunted by the subject, and in due course a verse was forthcoming.

Before young Isaac's death the brothers had changed their lodgings. The move was occasioned by an epileptic that lived with them whose fits had horrified Robert. In their new garret they lived with one James Kay, a furious Calvinist Scot, amongst whose library of books, and held in little esteem, were those two inevitably influential books, *The Seasons* and *Paradise Lost*. Robert borrowed them, read them, and a new poetic prospect opened before him. As surely as Wordsworth at Hawkshead, Bloomfield after his discovery of these poems became a dedicated spirit. Of *The Seasons* George said, "I never heard him give so much praise to any book as to that."

Three years after his first arrival in London an apprentice dispute caused Robert to return to the country for two months. He went to Sapiston where he stayed with his old employer, Mr. Austin. These months, which confirmed his memories of past joys and were heightened by the poetic awareness he had so recently received from Thomson, were probably the happiest, and certainly the most vivid, of his life. It was a return from exile to come again to the Suffolk fields he knew so well. He saw them at the age of seventeen with a more mature eye and an increased sensitivity. The holiday was short, but its influence was enormous.

On his return to London Robert was apprenticed to a ladies' shoe-maker, and while learning his trade many years slipped by. When he was twenty-one he invited the sons of his friend Mr. Austin for a visit to London. His letter to them, the earliest of his correspondence that is preserved, does not display any precocity, nor even the confidence of a man of the world. Although he had been seven years in London his life had been sheltered and unadventurous. "We must be very particular and not be out late of night," he warned his companions, "nor frequent any low lived places, and so long as we do so, there is no danger to be feared." Needless to add it was to be a cheap visit for Bloomfield was still desperately poor.

Two years later he found a comely young woman in Woolwich and married her, but his financial position had in no way improved. George describes his brother's difficulties:

Soon after he married, Robert told me, in a letter, that he had sold his fiddle, and got a wife. Like most poor men, he got a wife first, and had to get household stuff afterward. It took him some time to get out of ready-furnished lodgings. At length, by hard working, &c. he acquired a bed of his own, and hired the room up one pair of stairs, at 14, Bell-alley, Coleman-street. The landlord kindly gave him leave to sit and work in the light garret, two pair of stairs higher.

In this garret, amid six or seven other workmen, his active mind employed itself in composing *The Farmer's Boy*.

Although his surroundings were far from restful or conducive to thought, Robert committed whole sections of his poem to memory before he had a chance to write them down. The whole of *Winter* and most of *Autumn* were finished before he had put a single line on paper. It could not have been in the hope of fame or profit that he undertook this task. His ambitions were limited to the desire to present his mother with a printed copy of his poem, and before it had even been accepted for publication he assured his brother that he would not slacken off shoemaking on the chance of making five pounds out of *The Farmer's Boy*.

There was an urgency that made him write this poem which he never recaptured in his later work. It was a labour of love, a *credo*, and in a sense a gesture of defiance. He was proud of being, in his own words, a clodbred poet, and his poem was an act of disassociation from the urban world into which he had been forced. In spirit he was never a Londoner, though he spent more than half his life in that city, "When I said that I felt myself at home," he reflected in 1810 when his fame was assured and he was already contemplating returning to the land he loved, "I ought to have said that I wish'd the Country my home; and that radical first-planted principle in my composition can never be blotted out by London and all it can produce." The great city can have made singularly little impression on this pre-occupied shoemaker. He was not gifted with imagination, but his memory shielded him from uncongenial surroundings, and enabled him to transfer his mental life to those fields and woodlands where he had been most happy. "I have no leisure for any thing but thinking," he wrote at about this time. Memory was the only palliative to present misery.

The booksellers were not eager to print *The Farmer's Boy*. Bloomfield's manuscript was returned with a variety of excuses, and at last in despair of seeing it in print he gave it to his brother. In November 1798 George forwarded the poem to Capel Lofft, a gentleman of letters, eclectic and liberal in his tastes, whose benevolence not only to Bloomfield but to Kirke White earned him from Byron the stricture of being "the Maecenas of Shoemakers and preface-writer general to distressed versemen; a kind of gratis *accoucheur* to those who wish to be delivered of rhyme, but do not know how to bring forth."

Capel Lofft immediately realized the merit of *The Farmer's Boy*, and with enormous enthusiasm prepared the book for publication. He corrected the orthography and grammar, and, most important of all, found a bookseller who would produce it. "I have no doubt of its reception with the public," he said, "I have none of its going down to posterity with honour: which is not always the fate of productions which are popular in their day." Robert was content to leave the arrangements to Capel Lofft. He himself continued to make shoes, whistling and singing as he worked, and although he experienced at times the first pangs of the dejection and pain that were to haunt his later years he was tolerably content. To support a family on a journey-man's wage was no easy matter, but "there are times," he told his mother, "when the fire burns clear, and we all well, and our beer drawn good, and the candle fresh snuff'd, that I feel myself quite happy."

The publication of *The Farmer's Boy* in 1800 was an immediate success. Within three years 26,000 copies had been printed: a greater number of a new poem than had ever before been sold in so short a time. Like Duck, Bloomfield became a familiar name overnight, and he was sought out by the rich and the curious. Robert was able to send his mother a copy of the medium-sized edition of his poem, and reported to her that the Duke of Grafton, at the instigation of Capel Lofft, had invited him round and "gave me five guineas screwed up in a little bit of paper, and asked a thousand questions." The Duke was as enthusiastic as Lofft had been in the discovery of "a real untaught genius starting from our neighbourhood." He settled a small annuity of £15 on Bloomfield and obtained for him a job at the Seal Office.

At the end of the poet's first visit he was asked what books he would like. His reply was immediate: the poems of Burns. One of the ladies in the company added those of Mrs. Barbauld; but Bloomfield's choice was instinctively right. Burns was as fine a model as he could wish for, and although Robert knew himself to lack the intensity and inspiration of the Scottish poet, he clave to him rather than to the fashionable insipidities of Mrs. Barbauld. Both the success of Burns's genius and the wreckage of his life were constantly in Bloomfield's mind. Writing to the Earl of Buchan in 1802 he said: " 'Remember Burns' has been the watchword of my friends. *I do remember Burns*; but I am not Burns, neither have I his fire to fan, nor to quench, nor his passions to controul." But the example of Burns held fatal fascinations for the young poet. The self-identifications of Clare were only different in degree from the parallels that Bloomfield drew between Burns's condition and his own. Contemplating the worries that surrounded him he would reflect, "perhaps Bob Burns had some such cross-grain'd vexations as these, and strove to cure them by drinking." It is probable that Bloomfield did much the same.

Robert accepted his new position as the centre of London literary interest with great calmness and without becoming conceited. Although Charles Lamb considered him to be "a damn'd stupid hound in company," he was on the whole well received, and secured both patrons and friends amongst a wide circle of society. His letters show him to have been singularly unmoved by lionization. To his brother he reported in August 1801, without adding further comment, "my

Book affairs go on tolarably. I am getting acquainted with another Barronett. . . ."

Not everyone, however, was content to leave him to advance his own fame. His work was constantly interrupted by callers, and by post he received "many honourable testimonies of esteem from Strangers: Letters without a name, but filld with the most cordial advice, and allmost a parental anxiety for my safety under so great a share of publick applause." Pleasant as such interest might be to a man whom the world had hitherto always ignored, it was not helpful to his straitened financial position. To enter into society added fresh responsibilities and expenses, and Bloomfield was forced by the demands of his family to continue working when interruptions permitted. "My regular ernings are deminish'd," he complained to his brother,

in proportion to my corispondence and calling friends, my rent is a guinea pr. Month, which you know well cannot be supported by Journyman Shoe-making, under these circumstances I must either secure a regular income, or devour the produce of my litterary fame: This last I dont like to do, neither do I like mastering. I am very well off at present, but as the World is staring at me had not I better be seen busy ? ?

On the whole the world stared at Bloomfield and was gratified. Southey wrote enthusiastically about *The Farmer's Boy* in *The Critical Review*. Hazlitt, Rogers, Dyer, and a host of others added their praise. Lamb's was one of the few dissentient voices. Vernor and Hood, Bloomfield's publishers, pointed out that the merit of the poem was "contested pro & con by the Literary world," but despite this professional caution there were few who did not unreservedly acclaim, in Bernard Barton's words, "our own more chaste Theocritus."

In view of the unanimity of favourable opinion in 1800 and the little recognition it receives today, it will be useful at this juncture to examine in more detail the poem by which Bloomfield's poetic merits must be judged, *The Farmer's Boy*.

"I was determined that what I said on Farming should be EXPERI-MENTALLY true," wrote Bloomfield to explain the principle on which he had written *The Farmer's Boy*. Truth to events within his own experience is the most distinctive feature of the poem, and the accuracy with which he describes the minutiae of agricultural procedure and natural events is all the more astonishing when one considers the circumstances under which Bloomfield wrote. Thomson's *Seasons* was never far from him, but the debt was so immediately obvious (the structural plan of the two poems being identical) that he took pains to disassociate himself in treatment of subject from the manner of his great master. "No Alpine wonders thunder through my verse," he declared in the opening lines of *Spring*, obliquely referring to Thomson's love of florid, foreign descriptions. Although he is more homely in his seasonal pageant, and although verisimilitude is a poor substitute for vision, Bloomfield does succeed in capturing the spirit of the farm without being purely trivial. It is true that he lacks the flashes of genius that irradiate Thomson's turbid poem, but his average standard is surprisingly high. The couplet is handled with more freedom than in Duck's day; end-stopping is less inevitable, and there is a flexibility of diction and expression for which the credit must go not only to the poet but to the relaxing of poetic conventions during the later years of the eighteenth century.

The Farmer's Boy was not written autobiographically. It was well known that Giles was, in fact, a portrait of the poet in his youth, but none the less the lack of an insistent first person singular was conducive to better workmanship and less special pleading. Duck, in describing the arduous life of a tasker, could not detach himself from his work to view his whole surroundings with a proportionate vision. A thresher was not the mouthpiece for a composite picture of the countryside. No more was a farmer's boy; but Bloomfield used Giles only as a focal point to a larger background, much as Constable used figures in his farm-landscapes. Between Thomson and Bloomfield the difference in treatment, even of events common to both their poems, was so great that although many reviewers of *The Farmer's Boy* suggested the likelihood of parallelism, no specific accusations were lodged. Hazlitt, in a brilliant analysis of Bloomfield's poem in his *Lectures on the English Poets*, illustrates this.

Bloomfield very beautifully describes the lambs in springtime as racing round the hillocks of green turf: Thomson, in describing the same image, makes the mound of earth the remains of an old Roman encampment. Bloomfield never gets beyond his own experience; and that is somewhat confined. He gives the simple appearance of nature, but he gives it naked, shivering, and unclothed with the drapery of a moral imagination.

Despite his assertion that

> The Farmer's life displays in every part
> A moral lesson to the sensual heart,

Bloomfield was not a moral artist; Thomson, on the other hand, was intensely didactic. Hazlitt found a nakedness in Bloomfield's poem; certainly it is sparsely clad, but one must be grateful that he did not furbish his account with too much moral sentence. The infrequent instances of such additions are a salutary warning of weaknesses to which later he became sadly prone.

A peasant-poet is usually a humble man writing well within the orbit of his equally humble capacities. He is restricted in range, but not in excellence. *The Farmer's Boy* never attempts to strut or soar—indeed, Hazlitt considered that Bloomfield's Muse was not only rustic but menial in her aspect. This is not a condemnation so long as prosaism is avoided, and Bloomfield generally succeeded in retaining a thoroughly plain, but poetic, style. Towards the end of his life, in 1821, he wrote down what he considered to be bad ingredients in composition. These ingredients, when omitted, led to a form of writing in the language of ordinary life. Compound epithets, inversion, triplets, weak closing lines and archaic expressions he eschewed. Long passages in *The Farmer's Boy* contain no poetic diction, and sentences are linked together in so natural a way that "tills" and "ands" become tediously apparent.

The discipline of the couplet kept Bloomfield from straying far into the new, Wordsworthian theories of poetry. He had not the power of thought or invention to arrive at, or even to support, such controversial issues, and his popularity would certainly have waned if he had. In poetic technique Bloomfield was conservative but an individualist. Just as he prided himself on never meddling with politics or religion, so he refused to be associated with any school or style of literature. Wisely he desired to be known and judged as a farmer's boy: he sought no better name.

95

The association of Bloomfield with Wordsworth was not purely fortuitous. Although the Lake poet cannot be said to have influenced the poetry of the farmer's boy, Bloomfield's taste for simplicity of expression and accuracy of rural description made him amongst the first wholehearted admirers of Wordsworth's poetry outside the Lakers themselves. In 1801 Bloomfield was a far more esteemed and established poet than Wordsworth, and his opinions were not without influence. A hitherto unpublished letter to his brother George, dated April 19th, contains as a postscript, "I will soon send you Wordsworth's poems, if there is no poetry in them I will give up my pretention to feeling and Nature. I can trust you I think to be struck with them, first with their extreem simplicity, and then for what I before mention'd, *Nature*." Instinctive, natural taste has been claimed by a number of enthusiasts for a multitude of untaught geniuses. In this instance Bloomfield does seem to have immediately appreciated the merits of a poet who for many years laboured against fashion and prejudice. But he discovered in Wordsworth only what he had been striving to achieve himself.

Life on the farm has altered surprisingly little over the centuries. There is a universality of image in the language of nature that is the most constant and cohesive element in the flux of art and society. Giles, the farmer's boy in Bloomfield's poem, may in detail be performing different tasks from those that might fall upon him nowadays, but in general they are the same. Around him—and Giles is particularly conscious of external nature—nothing alters. The early morning chorus of birds still sings for those that rise as early as Giles, and if disturbed,

> Stopp'd in her song perchance the starting thrush
> Shook a white shower from the blackthorn bush.

With a delicate, Clare-like observation one can still watch how

> The small dust-colour'd beetle climbs with pain,
> O'er the smooth plantain-leaf, a spacious plain!
> Thence higher still, by countless steps convey'd,
> He gains the summit of a shiv'ring blade,
> And flirts his filmy wings, and looks around,
> Exulting in his distance from the ground.

96

Such minutely observed details are typical of Bloomfield's art. He possessed neither the scientific spirit of Erasmus Darwin, nor Thomson's flair for generalizing in his record of the natural world around him. Visual detail and precision were dear to him, but when first-hand experience failed he was timid of using his imagination. A year before *The Farmer's Boy* was published, Robert wrote to his brother, "I have read Gay's 'Trivia'; it descends to minute descriptions of London, more minute than mine do of the country; his minutiae must be more subject to change than mine, less dependent on nature." Even at the end of the century in which it was written the art of walking the streets of London had changed. Bloomfield, leaning on the immutability of the natural scene, hoped that his details would not suffer a similar fate to Gay's.

The cycle of the farming year opens with *Spring*, and the reader is quickly introduced to Giles, a boy not yet grown up into the cares of the world. Hard work did not bring with it the shades of the prison-house because it did not bring responsibility. There is something of the unconscious, primal freshness of the child of nature in Giles, which Duck's thresher, absorbed with the duties of the labouring round, never reflected.

> 'Twas thus with Giles: meek, fatherless, and poor:
> Labour his portion, but he felt no more;
> No stripes, no tyranny his steps pursued;
> His life was constant, cheerful servitude:
> Strange to the world, he wore a bashful look,
> The fields his study, Nature was his book.

The farmer, Giles's master, kept the young lad fully occupied. But the tasks were various and performed with good will—though not always efficiently. Giles was never so hard-pressed that he could not bend his hat into a telescope to watch the ascending lark, or fall asleep in the summer sun when he should have been bird-scaring. Duck, the day-labourer, analyses the tribulations of his work. Giles is not so introspective: he accepts the task and describes the scene resulting from it. His vision is far less confined than the thresher's, but no less accurate.

Spring ploughing offers Bloomfield an opportunity for the word-painting at which he excels.

With smiling brow the ploughman cleaves his way,
Draws his fresh parallels, and, wid'ning still,
Treads slow the heavy dale, or climbs the hill:
Strong on the wing his busy followers play,
Where writhing earth-worms meet th'unwelcome day;
Till all is changed, and hill and level down
Assume a livery of a sober brown;
Again disturb'd, when Giles with wearying strides
From ridge to ridge the ponderous harrow guides;
His heels deep sinking every step he goes,
Till dirt adhesive loads his clouted shoes.

There is a refreshing directness in such a passage that is seldom to be found so long-sustained even in Thomson's poem, and although there is no visionary quality in the verse there is a pictorial clarity that is entirely satisfying.

Mingled with such writing is a didactic element. Bloomfield overrides Giles to discourse on a variety of topics. The correct method of using scarecrows, the docking of horses' tails, and the new refinement that was fast imposing a caste system on rural society, all come up for discussion and judgment. On these matters Bloomfield had strong opinions and argues convincingly, but not in the manner of a farmer's boy. At times his appeal is purely pathetic: a description of lambs at play is followed by an indignant attack on the "murd'ring Butcher" whose abattoir is their destination.

Like the fond dove from fearful prison freed,
Each seems to say, "Come, let us try our speed;"
Away they scour, impetuous, ardent, strong,
The green turf trembling as they bound along;
Adown the slope, then up the hillock climb,
Where every molehill is a bed of thyme;
There panting stop; yet scarcely can refrain:
A bird, a leaf, will set them off again;
Or, if a gale with strength unusual blow,
Scatt'ring the wild-brier roses into snow,
Their little limbs increasing efforts try,
Like the torn flower the fair assemblage fly.
Ah, fallen rose! sad emblem of their doom;
Frail as thyself, they perish as they bloom!

Blomfield's freedom from poetic diction has already been commented upon. Usually this was nothing but an advantage, but in technical descriptions, such as that of butter-making, he is perhaps too exact. Facts are only one of the ingredients of poetry, and although Bloomfield was adept in handling material that the Augustans would have considered unsuitable for verse, he did not always load any of the rifts of his subject with ore. On occasions he deliberately wrote colloquially, and even humorously; his lines on Mary, the village beauty, stripped to the stays in the heat of harvesting, or the gander tyrannizing over the animals in the farmyard, show an ability to laugh that only Burns amongst peasant-poets possessed to the full.

Although the farmer himself is often unwilling to leave

> his elbow-chair
> His cool, brick floor, his pitcher and his ease,

Giles is at everybody's beck and call. He has only to pass the door of the dairy and

> The chatt'ring dairy-maid immersed in steam,
> Singing and scrubbing midst her milk and cream,
> Bawls out, "Go fetch the Cows."

Even so simple a task does not pass without comment. The reluctance of the cattle to leave their pasture is noted, and the fact that one cow invariably leads the rest. Each season is filled with a succession of such precise observations, and Bloomfield's verses are packed with country lore. Nor are his interests confined to the world of nature. He tells of a young mad girl in the village with a Wordsworthian curiosity in the subject, he visits the village church, which displays "the rude inelegance of Poverty," and discusses the deterioration of master and man relationships during the recent years. "Let labour have its due," he pleads, and tells how the spirit that prevails at harvest-home, when Distinction is in abeyance, was once common for more than one day in the year.

The seasonal labours naturally occupy the greater part of the poem. In early summer the hard-clodded ground is harrowed, and Giles is sent bird-scaring. Cobbett as a youth performed a similar task, and so, early in the new century, did Joseph Arch, the founder of the Agricultural Labourers' Union. The latter did not have such pleasant memories as Giles. At the age of nine, he recollected, he used to stand for twelve hours a day "in a new-sown field shivering on an empty stomach, while the cold wind blew and the chill rain poured down in torrents." Giles's easy, sleep-interspersed vigil is in strange contrast to Arch's; but Bloomfield was fortunate in having an humane employer. Both accounts are doubtless true, but at the time it was Bloomfield's that people wanted to hear about.

Hay-making receives only a short mention, and this omission prompted an uneducated farmer at Croydon, in Surrey, to write *An Appendix to the Season of Spring, in the Rural Poem, "The Farmer's Boy."* Joseph Holland, the author, published this poem locally in 1806, and, in contrast to Duck, it was the only book of acknowledged imitation that Bloomfield inspired.

The harvest is the principal event in *Summer*, and the gaiety and enjoyment with which everyone participates is more in the spirit of Thomson than Duck. But it is not an idyll, and "the sov'reign cordial, home-brew'd ale" quenches thirsts that have been raised by hard and unsparing work.

Giles's occupations during the autumn are equally various. The pigs are sent out to forage for acorns in the unenclosed woodlands, and winter wheat is sown. Once again Giles becomes a bird-scarer; he diverts himself this time by building a hut—very much as Bevis, or any country child might do—and cooks sloes and rose-hips over a little fire.

> o'er the flame the sputt'ring fruit he rests,
> Placing green sods to seat the coming guests;
> His guests by promise; playmates young and gay:—
> But ah! fresh pastimes lure their steps away!
> He sweeps his hearth, and homeward looks in vain,
> Till feeling Disappointment's cruel pain,
> His fairy revels are exchanged for rage,
> His banquet marr'd, grown dull his hermitage.

During the winter fodder must be provided for the cattle, and Giles is employed carting turnips, a newly-introduced root crop, to the beasts in the frozen fields. For those in the stalls hay needed to be carried;

> Deep-plunging cows their rustling feast enjoy,
> And snatch sweet mouthfuls from the passing boy,
> Who moves unseen beneath his trailing load,
> Fills the tall racks, and leaves a scatter'd road.

Giles himself was too young for the most arduous task of the winter season, but it is a job that Duck had fully described before him—threshing. Well into the evening the threshing-floor resounds with noise.

> Though night approaching bids for rest prepare,
> Still the flail echoes through the frosty air,
> Nor stops till deepest shades of darkness come,
> Sending at length the weary labourer home.

Daylight does not last long in winter-time; after dark there are more sinister happenings. The shepherd is on guard against the roaming dog that has been worrying his sheep, and Giles, walking down a narrow lane, is terrified by the sight of

> A grisly Spectre, clothed in silver-grey,
> Around whose feet the waving shadows play,

—an apparition that is happily discovered to be an old ash-tree.

The seasons again change, and the first lambs herald a new spring. Although the poem ends here, the theme can never end, and Bloomfield more than any other cyclical poet recognizes the recurrence of the fundamental natural force that presses the sap through the hedgerows and the flowers from the earth. Giles, perceiving the new year "returning as the wheel returns," views it with joy.

> Another Spring! His heart exulting cries,
> Another Year.

"The public taste hangs like a millstone round the neck of all original genius that does not conform to established and exclusive models," declared Hazlitt. It was Thomson who had paved the way for Bloomfield's success, and it is in connection with his study of *The Seasons* that Hazlitt took the opportunity of including *The Farmer's Boy* amongst the greater poems in his *Lectures on the English Poets*. In Hazlitt's eyes the association was not invidious. He admired the "delicacy, faithfulness and *naïveté*" of Bloomfield's poem, and bestowed on it the shrewdest criticism that it was to obtain. "We cannot expect from original genius alone," he continued, "without education, in modern and more artificial periods, the same bold and independent results as in former periods." Whether those "former periods" lay in the romantic imagination, or whether Hazlitt is referring to writers such as Langland, whose poems have come to us unburdened by biography, is not clear; but the reasons Hazlitt gives for his statement are interesting.

Although the original genius was free from the trammels of custom and other men's ideas, he tended to be oppressed by his situation. Advantages that he did not possess and glory that he did not share made him conscious and imitative of his more fortunate, but often less talented, brothers in verse; whereas his natural inclination should have led him to reap the rich harvest of his own original inspiration— a harvest the more precious for being hitherto untouched. Another reason that Hazlitt advanced to explain the ultimate failure of original genius was that such genius needed to be supported by "a corresponding state of manners, passions, and religious belief." Against such a judgment Bloomfield cannot stand; nor for that matter could any English untutored poet. Only Burns and Iolo Morganwg might be defended by these critical standards.

The tenor of Hazlitt's criticism was nevertheless highly favourable, though he realized the weakness inherent in Bloomfield's poem. Not so did Dr. Nathan Drake, who did not consider "any production can be put in competition with it since the days of Theocritus." Dr. Drake's was not an isolated opinion, and it is, therefore, refreshing to find Lamb downright in his condemnation. Writing to his friend Manning on November 3, 1800, he adds in a postscript,

You ask me about the *Farmer's Boy*. Don't you think the fellow who wrote it (who is a shoemaker) has a poor mind? Don't you find he is always silly about *poor Giles*, and those abject kind of phrases, which mark a man that looks up to wealth? None of Burns's poet dignity. What do you think? I have just opened him; but he makes me sick.

Lamb's views have, perhaps, been vindicated by the steady decline of Bloomfield's verse in public regard; but it is too hot-blooded a criticism to be accepted without reserve. It contains an immediate perception of weaknesses that Hazlitt was later to generalize in his lecture on Thomson and Crabbe, but it is blind to many undeniable merits that the poem possesses.

The opinion of most of Bloomfield's distinguished contemporaries must have been exceedingly gratifying to him. Capel Lofft was energetic in promoting interest in a book that cast not a little reflected glory on himself. George Dyer, to whom Lofft had sent a copy, wrote back at some length in praise of the poem.

Yes Sir, I have read *The Farmer's Boy*, and intend to read it over and over again some time hence. *The Farmer's Boy* appears to me a truly original and beautiful poem. It recalled to my mind those ages and those countries in which the poet and the shepherd were more naturally united, and under those circumstances some of the earliest Scotch Ballads were written, and they please us because they breathe the language of nature and speak to the heart. . . . I perceive no fopperies—no meretricious ornaments, no language of bigotry and enthusiasm in Bloomfield.

Amongst the reviewers Southey, writing in *The Critical Review*, was conspicuous for his encouragement and praise. "This poem abounds with beautiful lines of accurate and minute description," he declared. Lofft himself, in a note to George Bloomfield was, at least at the time of publication, unreserved in his respect. "His want of Education (what is generally so called) has had its advantages, if he had been learned it would not have been possible that he should have produced so purely original a poem." Like Hannah More with her milkwoman, Lofft changed his tune when Bloomfield showed the first stirrings of an independent spirit.

Fame and fortune did not make Bloomfield happy. His financial affairs worried and confused him, the expenses of his new position in society, his desire to help his relations and the constant ill-health that dogged both him and his family, all combined to depress him. "I think a man really mad is far happier than one who has this dastardly sinking of the soul, and retains his reason seemingly for no other purpose than to prove its weakness," he confessed to his brother in

August 1801; and again, "O Lord! what a poor creature is Man! and of Men what a poor creature is a Bloomfield." As the years passed his letters become less and less concerned with affairs of the spirit. His eagerness in the discovery of poetry, and the critical opinions that he exchanged with his brother die away. Instead there are recurrent accounts of the pain in his loins, his rheumatism and his migraine. Hypochondria and a morbid interest in his own health dominate his correspondence.

Bloomfield's wife, who might have lifted his spirits, had become an ardent disciple of Joanna Southcott. He himself hated his new employment at the Seal Office, and the insinuations he overheard that his job was a poet's sinecure. He wanted to write, but had neither the inspiration nor the time. His days were filled with callers, visits to the printers and other worries. "I have no time to write down my Rhimes," he told his brother, "I have enough on my mind to craze a saint."

To add to his distress a quarrel developed with Capel Lofft. Bloomfield was unwilling to enter into it, but was caught between his printer and his patron. Certain eulogistic notes, by Lofft and others, were to have been inserted in front of the individual poems in the new edition of Bloomfield's work. Robert claimed that this prejudiced independent judgment of the poems, and was harmful to his reputation. He asked that they might be printed at the end of the book. Lofft, who was alone in being aggrieved, accused Bloomfield of trying to squeeze him out. In fact nothing could have been farther from the truth. Capel Lofft received nothing but the sincerest praise and gratitude in both the public and the private writings of Bloomfield. The quarrel made further relationships very strained, but Robert never ceased to regret the estrangement of his "first great friend Mr. Lofft."

Robert Bloomfield never held those radical principles that some of his critics ascribed to him. In his poetry he recorded facts and not opinions, except on certain humanitarian subjects such as cruelty to horses. In his life, however, he did not cease to express the opinions, and plead the causes, of the class from which he sprang. On the subject of illiteracy he put forward his views, as might be expected, with considerable force. A remark by a Mr. Windham had offended him, and on May 30, 1802 Bloomfield wrote, the *common people* of his native country, are a rough set no doubt, but I dislike the doctrine of keeping them in their dirt, for though it holds good as to the preservation of potatoes, it would be no grateful reflection to good minds to know that a man's natural abilities had been smother'd for want of beeing able to read and write. How can we consistently praise the inestimable blessing of letters and not wish to extend it? Or why should the Great and the Wealthy confine the probable production of intelectual excelence to their own class, and exclude, by withholding the polish, all that might amongst the poor by nature be intended to be Newton's and Locke's?

That same month he wrote to Mr. Pratt, acknowledging his poem, *Bread*, in terms that would not have pleased his patrons. "To see one class of the community grow immencely rich at the expence of another, to me allways argue'd an inefficiency in the Laws of this or any Country where it happens."

Bloomfield was not given to flattery, but neither was he by nature a reformer. Early in his career as a poet he received and followed some excellent advice from the Duke of Grafton; and two years before his death he was able to assert "that out of all my numerous friends, none have got even a Sonnet from me; flattery is a poor way of paying debts." Duck would have profited from a similar determination. It was, perhaps, Bloomfield's noticeable silence in the matter of verse tributes, and his similar reticence in acknowledging the benefits of the Government or the Church, that caused it to be widely supposed that he had "imbibed both Deistical and Republican principles." In 1821 his good friend Mr. Baker wrote imploring him to deny the rumours that were having a damaging effect on his reputation. In his reply Bloomfield remarked that the accusations were only half the story. Cobbett, far from thinking him a republican, considered that Robert had been "taken in tow" by the Government to prevent him writing in favour of the people. Radical reformers, even when they championed the rural poor, met with no support from Bloomfield. "Cobbet and Hunt are men whom I would not trust with power," he told Baker, "they are too eager to obtain it. Universal suffrage is an impracticable piece of nonsense."

At the end of 1801 Bloomfield was anxiously awaiting the publication of his second book, *Rural Tales*. "No dying Lover in a romance ever long'd for the bridal-day more sincerely or fervently than I do for the birth of my Voll^m." This collection of shorter, principally narrative, poems was again kindly received by the critics. Southey considered the standard to be as high as *The Farmer's Boy*, and Clare, in a letter written in 1825, after Bloomfield's death, was especially attracted by one of the ballads in this collection. Recollecting all that he knew of a man whom he had never met, but whose genius he admired, Clare wrote, in his usual unpunctuated fashion,

he dyed ripe for immortality and had he written nothing else but "Richard and Kate" that fine picture of Rural Life were sufficient to establish his name as the English Theocritus and the first of Rural Bards in this country and as Fashion (that feeble substitute for fame) had nothing to do in his exaltation its neglect will have nothing to affect his memory it is built on a more solid foundation and time will bring its own reward to the "Farmers Boy."

There is little that would attract a reader today in these sentimental anecdotes of idealized rural life. Their recitation moved Bloomfield to tears, but they are undistinguished poems, and, unlike *The Farmer's Boy*, might have been written by a townsman. Like Duck, Bloomfield's limited powers made him a one-poem man. The more he attempted to recapture his lost Muse, the farther he strayed into mediocrity. Towards the end of his poetic career he wrote,

I sometimes dream that I shall one day venture again before the public, something in my old manner, some Country tales, and spiced with love and courtship might yet please, for Rural life by the art of Cooking may be made a relishing and high flavour'd dish, whatever it may be in reality.

A clue to his inspirational failure may be seen in this confession. When he wrote *The Farmer's Boy* no "cooking" was required. Something of the visionary gleam was still with him. When he no longer found nature sufficient in herself, and had recourse to artifices to render her attractive, he ceased to be a country poet and became a hack.

Although *Rural Tales* was very far from being a failure, the attention paid to each subsequent volume was less. Bloomfield strayed from poetry to write children's stories and a play, *Hazelwood Hall*, despite an avowed ignorance of "the 'Dramatic unities,' or of what is call'd 'Stage effect.'" But his pen grew less willing as his hypochondria increased. In his letters he constantly talked of the large sums of money he was earning. At the same time he was always in a state of near-insolvency. His misfortunes were not entirely imaginary. In 1811 his publisher, Hood, died and his successor sold most of Bloomfield's copyrights before himself going bankrupt. By his own estimation Robert lost nearly £300 from this stroke of ill-fortune.

The proceeds from his poems were never the only source of Bloomfield's income. After he had abandoned his job at the Seal Office he started bookselling; but this project failed, and he returned for a while to his original trade of shoemaking. No longer was his temperament suited to a journeyman's occupation; neither, he considered, was his health. Apart from the making of verses the only trade he consistently plied was the manufacture of aeolian harps. In July 1807 he complained to his brother of the "accumulating plagues which arise from my Harp trade . . . and from the unseasonable and impudand visits of the vain, and the interested, and the curious, taking up my time, inviting me to Dinner etc. etc." Seventeen years later amongst his personal effects auctioned after his death were six unfinished aeolian harps; a testimony, perhaps, to the number of callers who had distracted him.

There were bright moments in the gloom that enveloped his years of fame. Now and then he would escape from his wife and explore the countryside. In 1803 he was astonished at the romantic prospects around Dorking: Leith Hill and Box Hill were the highest eminences he had ever seen. For some years he made a similar expedition each summer, either alone or with friends. The most memorable of these, in 1807, was to the West Country, and he published a record in verse of all that he had seen. It did not come easily. He wrote and rewrote, submitted his manuscripts to criticism and then started again. His impressions were strong enough, but he had lost the ability to record them spontaneously. The spirit of the topographer—the guide-book writer rather than the poet—fills his pages. The horizons that opened before him were too wide, too superficially seen, to yield any profitable meditation. Into a verse-letter, written in little more than an octosyllabic jingle, he attempted to compress the history, geography, and poetic impulses of the March-lands. In days when travel was still restricted there may have been a good excuse (though not a poetic one) for such a commentary, but the charm was ephemeral and the prosaism of the work is only emphasized by Bloomfield's frequent use of footnotes to explain facts otherwise too cumbersome to be included.

The later years of Bloomfield's life, and the further books of poetry that he produced in his constant efforts to flog his failing Muse, are best passed over briefly. His inspiration had been choked by success. Like Clare and Burns drink, ill-health and the deceptive dawn of untroubled days undermined the years of his fame. *Good Tidings*, a poem written to advance the cause of Jenner's then controversial vaccine, *Wild Flowers*, and *May-Day with the Muses* did nothing to advance his reputation. Sentiment drifted with little struggle into sentimentality, and rhyming became a laborious technique without the urgency of self-expression.

In 1812 the poet, impecunious and London-sick, moved out of the city to Shefford, a village in Bedfordshire. The rent of his cottage was covered by the annuity that he had begged the new Duke of Grafton to renew. But even the reduced expenses of a country life proved too great for his straitened resources. Within four years an appeal was published soliciting contributions from the friends and admirers of Robert Bloomfield. A trust fund was formed, from which before long Robert was desirous of drawing the capital. It was not only that he was improvident; his family and many of his relatives received more assistance than he was capable of giving, and Bloomfield's popularity was not enhanced amongst his benefactors by the discovery that the money they had contributed towards his welfare had been passed on to some poor dependent.

In 1817 the Duke of Grafton, after some prompting, paid Bloomfield's annuity, with a chilly regret "that Mr. B's muse should have been so long silent." That same year Crabbe met him during a visit to London. In his journal for July 3rd he remarked, "he had better rested as a shoemaker, or even a farmer's boy; for he would have been a farmer perhaps in time, and now he is an unfortunate poet. By the way, indiscretion did much." Bloomfield's fellow East Anglian was a man who had himself experienced the misery of poverty and want; it is therefore on a more charitable note that he left him: "he is, however, to be pitied and assisted." But it could have been of little consolation to Bloomfield, the sale of whose own poems had much diminished, to learn "that Murray gave parson Crabb 3 thousand pounds for his Tales."

Crabbe did not become a spokesman for the peasantry—or, more accurately, for the poor people of village and borough—until he had entirely severed his own bonds of poverty. During the days when he shared his bed with a ploughboy or pawned his last belongings in order to keep alive in London his writings contained nothing to distinguish them from the run of the mill verses of his day. True to the tradition of poetry in which he was reared he wrote his reports upon completed experience. The same thought, viewed by Clare as an intuitive desire,

> I long for scenes where man has never trod,

is recorded by Crabbe as an accomplished pleasure,

> I loved to walk where none had walk'd before.

The difference between the two approaches is remarkable, and even more curious when one considers that Clare's desire for solitude was to gain greater communion with God. Crabbe's indulgence is an intellectual whimsey, his regard for truth never permitting him to crusade in the realms of the spirit. Keats's description of his own and Byron's poetry is analogous here: "There is this great difference between us. He describes what he sees—I describe what I imagine. Mine is the hardest task."

In Crabbe's later verses, when the telling of tales became the major preoccupation of his pen, and disenchantment had been sobered down to a gentle pity, there is a noticeable lack of anagogical interpretation in his stories. Without the onion-layers of symbolism the critical reader may find the simple narration of verse-anecdotes are thin even to pointlessness. Crabbe was a good self-critic when he surveyed his works, shorn of all emotions beyond pity, impervious to the beguilements of music and beauty, and dubbed it "poetry without an atmosphere."

There is so much that has been and might be written about Crabbe that it is important in this brief survey to select only those aspects of his life and work that are germane to the subject of this book. When Clare wrote to his friend and fellow-poet Allan Cunningham about Crabbe we find him standing a little on his dignity, and certainly not acknowledging Crabbe to be a man of his own class.

Crabbe writes about the peasantry as much like the Magistrate as the Poet. He is determined to show you their worst side: and as to their simple pleasures and pastoral feelings, he knows little or nothing about them compared to the other [Robert Bloomfield], who not only lived amongst them, but felt and shared the pastoral pleasures with the peasantry of whom he sung.

Although such diverse tastes as those of Wordsworth and Dr. Johnson found pleasure in the verses of Crabbe, he was to receive no approbation from those folk from whose stock he had risen and whose way of life he attempted to record. It is difficult to doubt the veracity of Crabbe's picture (granting, of course, the magisterial attitude), but it seems that "the real picture of the poor" was the last thing that the poor poet wished to have exposed. The happiness and hopes of life which we often suspect to be the coloured threads of desire, may, when spun by the lowliest of our articulate poets, be themselves the very fabric of their poetry. For if the poet is down and out he cannot write down without denegration, and none but the most shameless poetaster (Tatersal the bricklayer, for instance) would attempt to do so. Burns, Bloomfield, and Clare found splendours and nobility in the same miseries that Crabbe was busy meticulously delineating.

The opening lines of *The Village* are nowadays the verses by which Crabbe is best known, when in his indignation he launches his most bitter attack at the pathetic or parblind effusions of pastoral poetry.

> Yes, thus the Muses sing of happy swains,
> Because the Muses never knew their pains:
> They boast their peasants' pipes; but peasants now
> Resign their pipes and plod behind the plough;
> And few, amid the rural-tribe, have time
> To number syllables, and play with rhyme;

Those peasants who had not utterly laid by their pipes did not appreciate his solicitude. They mistrusted him when they never questioned Thomson.

Hazlitt who, in Keats's words, "gave Crabbe an unmerciful licking" in his lecture on Thomson and Cowper, seized upon the inertness of Crabbe's writing, his "*still life* of tragedy," as a fundamental weakness. There was justification in doing so, but the fault was caused, not by lack of interest in, or knowledge of, his subject as Clare would have believed, but by his literary technique. He was a moral poet and he preached the evils of life, leaving to the reader the comparison with the good. Beauty, far from being correlative, was ancillary to truth. When Hazlitt declared that Crabbe's poetry bore the same relation to actual life that a stuffed cat in a glass case did to the real one purring on the hearth, he was comparing the green in nature to the green in literature, with which, as we have seen, Crabbe was not concerned. He was concerned with delineation, the etched precision of Bewick or Audubon, as an aid to identification.

Few men who have succeeded in breaking through the obscurity of their birth have retained so little trace of their origin. His pictures show Crabbe to have had a rugged, kindly face, expressive and wide-mouthed, with no trace of the terrible early years in London disturbing the serenity of middle-life. The written descriptions we have of him seldom refer to any quaint provincialisms or gaucheries that might mark the son of a collector of salt-duties. Once Burke had befriended him Crabbe seems to have slipped naturally and easily into society, and to have been accepted by everyone except those with whom he grew up. In the years of his established fame after the death of his wife, when youth and good company rivalled the attractions of botanizing, Crabbe paid a visit to one of his most distinguished admirers, Sir Walter Scott, and during the entertainment made the acquaintance of a truly unsophisticated peasant-poet, James Hogg, the Ettrick shepherd, who "amused him much by calling for a can of ale, while champagne and claret, and other choice wines were in full circulation." Towards a fellow-man who had also triumphed over lowly birth Crabbe recognized no deeper bond, nor experienced any associative impulse.

Saeva indignatio is an aristocratic emotion, a haughtiness that in the truly great is fused with a swift and generous love. The quickest change of mood, the sun after the storm-cloud, does not imply indecision but a noble flexibility in the April weather of the intellect. The mind must be young in spirit to conceive it, however old it may be in wisdom. Crabbe never seems to have been young in anger. Even the poems he wrote when he was scarcely more than a boy have a grave, middle-aged air about them. He never relaxed or attempted familiarity with his Muse. In purpose his poetry was moral, in manner it was often pontifical, and this last quality was a new departure for anyone claiming kinship with the peasant-poets of any tongue. When peasants write verse "in the manner of art" they do so in humility and without dogma. Often they are experimental, seldom are they assured. Their successes can be directly connected to their verve—one might almost claim, to their boyishness. The sophisticated youthfulness mentioned above is, of course, as alien an emotion as Crabbe's earnest wrath: so alien that imitation was never attempted by any peasant-poet. When their anger was raised in poetry it took the form either of a circumstantially precise explanation of the injury in question (Bloomfield, for example, on the docking of horses' tails), or in those rare cases when the poet possessed enough self-confidence to let his public laugh with him (Burns springs immediately to mind), a boisterous mockery.

Youth and nature walk hand in hand. The bucolic setting, like Byzantium, is not a country for old men. We have already seen that it is young poets who have wandered most happily and affectionately out of doors, and although Wordsworth and Barnes continued in old age to write poetry that owed its main springs to external nature, it was for the most part a vision of reflected light in the eyes of young lovers, and of conjured memories of childhood.

Edwin, the hero of Beattie's poem, *The Minstrel*, shows admirably how the progress of a "natural" genius, "a shepherd-swain, a man of low degree," could be a conscious descent down the very path that Wordsworth was struggling up. In his earliest youth Edwin was a sensitive, introspective youth—a highland counterpart of the poet Clare.

> Silent when glad; affectionate, though shy;
> And now his look was most demurely sad;
> And now he laugh'd aloud, yet none knew why.
> The neighbours stared and sigh'd, yet bless'd the lad;
> Some deem'd him wondrous wise, and some believed him mad.

He was a child of the romantic imagination with a predilection towards Walpolian Gothic. The metamorphosis is curious, although after following the careers of Duck and Bloomfield it cannot be called surprising. In the second part of the poem Edwin encounters a recluse, representing a superior intelligence, who instructs the youth to "Curb Imagination's lawless rage," to appreciate that "Fancy enervates, while it sooths, the heart," and to cultivate (by way of an alternative) philosophy. The effect of this teaching may be seen in Edwin's poetry.

> Of late, with cumbersome, though pompous show,
> Edwin would oft his flowery rhyme deface,
> Through ardour to adorn; but Nature now
> To his experienced eye a modest grace
> Presents, where Ornament the second place
> Holds, to intrinsick worth and just design
> Subservient still. Simplicity apace
> Tempers his rage: he owns her charm divine,
> And clears th'ambiguous phrase, and lops th'unwieldy line.

This digression into the work of a Scots poet who, although poorly born, spent much of his life as Professor of Moral Philosophy at Aberdeen University, only reinforces an earlier generalization that youth and nature are interrelated. It is to the simple vision of Wordsworth or Blake that we are accustomed to turn to support such an opinion; but the Romantic Movement taught peasants so little and the Augustans so much that Beattie's poetical autobiography has a value as a working pattern for the development and self-improvement of young peasant-poets to which *The Prelude* cannot compare.

When a poet wore the badge of his vocation in his published works his readers became restive if he indulged in original thought or neglected the already known and familiar landscape. Those who were deceived by the "National Work" that purported to come from the pens of the brothers Whistlecraft (and despite the transparency of the ruse there were not a few) were astonished not, as they well might have been, at the ingenuity of the metre or the blandness of expression in Frere's poem, but at the presumptuousness of the harness-makers in failing to enter the mansion of the Muses through the tradesmen's door.

It was understandable. If a man proclaimed himself uneducated no reader of his poems minded being indulgent; but the very suspicion of superior learning—or in the case of a Wordsworthian "natural" mystic, of superior and baffling simplicity—would irk any reader who considered himself culturally and educationally more advanced than the author. It was not surprising that Frere's poem was never a great success. It had a stigma of cleverness without the assurance of good breeding; and besides, it never succeeded in telling a story.

In the early years of the nineteenth century only the mild didacticism of Rogers or of Bowles could stand alongside the narrative verse of Scott, Byron, and Crabbe in public esteem. *The Farmer's Boy*, the most popular of all poems written by English peasant-poets, achieved its success by appealing both to those who liked a good story and to those who appreciated the most humble and unassuming of moral conclusions. No fortunes were made by poets whose craft relied upon sense-impression or introspective analysis. An occasional critic of acute perception or generous disposition could not persuade the public that occupational verse warranted particular attention. Wars and the failure of harvest flooded the land with destitution; the drift into the towns and the soliciting of patronage were commonplace and only caused purse-strings to be drawn tighter. Capel Lofft and the ever-charitable Southey deserve especial mention at this time for their constant encouragement and assistance of inexperienced poets. That Bloomfield or Henry Kirke White are even known to us today is entirely due to their recognition of the genius in these unfortunate youths.

Like most of the poorly-born poets of his generation Kirke White published his first poems in the columns of the local paper. The spread of provincial journalism provided forums of inestimable value to many a promising writer, and made the discovery of real talent less haphazard than it had been in Duck's time. Capel Lofft's encouragement and his own zeal for learning persuaded White, the son of a Nottingham butcher, to acquire enough education to devote himself entirely to the pursuit of literature. "Poetry," he confided in a letter to Lofft, "has been to me something more than amusement; it has been a cheering companion when I have had no other to fly to, and a delightful solace when consolation has been in some measure needful." It may be judged by the tone of his letter that White was temperamentally melancholy, but driven from within (as has been the case with so many consumptive and short-lived geniuses) by a furious and impatient will. The poems in *Clifton Grove*, the small volume that he published in 1803 in order to secure the money necessary to take him to Cambridge, have a plaintive, pityingly elegiac ring about them, unnatural in so young a writer. Even at the age of fourteen, when he wrote his poem *Childhood*, he seems to be shrinking from the self-discipline and intense study to which he dedicated his short and already doomed life. Addressing the mistress of the Dame's School where he was first taught, he cried,

> Oh! had the venerable matron thought
> Of all the ills by talent often brought;
> Could she have seen me when revolving years
> Had brought me deeper in the vale of tears,
> Then had she wept, and wished my wayward fate
> Had been a lowlier, an unlettered state;
> Wished that, remote from worldly woes and strife,
> Unknown, unheard, I might have passed through life.

Chatterton in his disillusionment or Clare insane might understandably have voiced such a desire. Kirke White, who was young and in comparatively untroubled circumstances, displays a terrible and morbid precocity.

As with Crabbe and the best amongst the ill-educated writers who have chosen a sophisticated medium of expression, it is the intensity of feeling and urgency with which the poet cries out to be heard that is arresting in *Clifton Grove*; the niceties of composition, as the unfavourable remarks in *The Monthly Review* point out, are lacking. But Southey saw merit in the collection, and together with Capel Lofft he succeeded in obtaining an entrance for Kirke White into Cambridge. The end was not long in coming. Weakened by recurring illnesses and never pausing in his ardour for study to recruit his strength, the consumption that he had never allowed to deflect him from his work destroyed him in his twenty-second year.

The new century was no kinder to its poets than the old. Probably it was harsher, for the changes in social structure allowed no place for struggling poets—nor, necessarily, for established ones. A private income or a benefice seemed increasingly desirable before launching oneself into literature. After the Napoleonic Wars more poetry seemed to be written, and less read, than ever before. Even with a patron, as we have seen in Kirke White, advancement was not easy. Without one it must have been well-nigh impossible. We know only of those who succeeded to some extent in establishing themselves through publication; it is fruitless (but disturbing) to speculate on those who failed. The number of talented poets who have been lost, especially in rural areas, through lack of opportunity cannot be told, but we know that it was largely by luck that Duck, Bloomfield, and Clare came first to be printed.

Crabbe knew what a gamble it was. He could see a literate public growing so large that it accepted no responsibility for individual authors. But although Crabbe sold his poems, he could neither sell his opinions nor prevent poor poets from dazzling themselves with the hope of fame.

John Clare

A silent man in life's affairs,
A thinker from a boy,
A peasant in his daily cares,
A poet in his joy.

JOHN CLARE: *The Peasant Poet*

"We have no right to question the genius for want of the *gentility*,"
Hazlitt once remarked; yet this will inevitably be a consideration in
assessing any man as a purely peasant-poet. The sympathetic curiosity
that Southey, for example, tried to exploit when placing before the
public the attempts in verse of an old servant, and even the excitement
of novelty that poems written by a farmer's boy stirred up, have no
bearing at all on the excellence of a poet. If any of the figures who fill
these pages are to be considered as more than nine-day wonders, it
must be on account of their intrinsic poetic worth, not because of their
various humble employments. That one troubles to consider even
briefly the lives of men and women whom one has already judged as
poetasters may be explained by a Johnsonian wonderment not that
their verses were ill-done, but that they were done at all. But there are
other considerations. Setting aside literary criteria, uneducated poetry
marks a record of human endeavour, and, more pertinent to this
particular study, acts as a foil to those rare spirits of high genius whose
works plead for their own immortality without the advocacy of
biography. A poet of such distinction is John Clare.

Like other versifiers in similar circumstances, Clare found it invidious
to be known as a peasant-poet. The word "peasant" came to be
treated as a modification of "poet," and Clare had no wish for indulgence. After his first book had brought him some fame, he tried to
establish his reputation with more refined verses, written under a
pseudonym, often in imitation of the manner of other poets. With
him such attempts were little more than freaks, but for poets like

Duck and Bloomfield the cultivation of correctness became an end in itself.

To achieve an unaffected simplicity, both of diction and of thought, without incurring the opprobrium of archness or inanity, might be thought to be easier for a man such as Clare who

> found the poems in the fields,
> And only wrote them down,

than for writers of more studied innocence like Wordsworth or Barnes. Clare is alone amongst English poets who have been born field-labourers in retaining, and even sharpening, throughout his life a sensitive and accurate observation of all that passes in the quiet world of nature. "To look on Nature with a poetic eye magnifies the pleasure, she herself being the essence and soul of Poesy," he wrote, expressing instinctively the argument which the Lake School was propounding against the conventions and traditions that divorced poetry from the very sources of its inspiration.

In one respect this attitude of Clare's betrayed his lack of imagination. All he wrote, with the understandable exception of certain asylum poems, was firmly based on the reality of the physical world around him. He lacked the vision of Wordsworth, who used nature as a medium of interpretation to plumb the deeper mysteries beyond. Clare was never a philosopher of nature, but he unconsciously possessed much of the elemental clarity for which the greater poet strove. The very precision of Clare's observations from nature, and his fidelity to the record of his senses, is at once the delight and the weakness of his poetry. The delight is obvious from a cursory glance at his lyrics; the weakness lies in its exclusiveness. Such purity of vision—hardly a poet in the language has higher claims—left no opportunities for "the shaping spirit" to mingle with and translate the factual observation.

Wordsworth, who "saw by glimpses," grasped intuitively after the sublime; but Clare, possessing to the full those primary qualifications that Wordsworth demanded of a poet, that he should possess "more than usual organic sensibility," and that his poetry should be "the spontaneous overflow of powerful feelings," could not "think long and deeply" beyond the object itself. This was an inevitable defect, and sprang from the very refinement of Clare's own vision. Wordsworth himself was inferior to Clare in the spontaneity of his thought, and betrayed it by an unconscious didacticism. This element Clare seems never to have noticed, for he records in his diary, "when I first began to read poetry I disliked Wordsworth because I heard he was disliked; and I was astonished when I looked into him to find my mistaken pleasure in being delighted and finding him so natural and beautiful."

Clare's tenacity in continuing to write as he wished, from the heart, and not as others wished him to, from the head, is particularly interesting for the light it throws on his theory of poetry. "I wrote because it pleased me in sorrow, and when happy it makes me happier," he said, and this spirit, a dignified melancholy or rapturous joy, gives his poetry a deceptive air of leisurely country pleasures; whereas in reality, as Crabbe well realized,

> few, amid the rural-tribe, have time
> To number syllables, and play with rhyme.

Many of his friends, amongst them Darley, advised Clare not to be content with merely descriptive verse, and told him to infuse a more dramatic spirit. "The hooks with which you have hitherto fished for praise in the ocean of literature, have not been garnished with *live-bait*; and none can get a bite without it." But Clare was stubbornly independent of the criticism of his contemporaries. Poetry was too personal a matter to be consciously subjected to outside influence. "The Soul," Clare believed, "lies buried in the ink that writes." Unconsciously, as we shall see, Clare constantly echoed the poets whom he had read and admired, from the early imitations of Thomson to the final self-identification with Byron.

But these were no more than superficial debts; the essential poet in Clare owed no allegiance except to Love and Nature. These forces alone could keep him writing for three days and nights without intermission, and when his speech and prose style betrayed the madness of his brain, these forces were strong enough to control the lucidity of his verse. Lamb's advice, though well intended, to "transport Arcadia to Helpstone," was, therefore, unnecessary. Helpstone, the village on the borders of the Fen country where Clare was born, was already Arcadian to him—every inch of it a potential poem.

The urgency of self-expression is not apparent in Clare's verse; yet the tragedy of his impoverished existence, the hopelessness of his prospects, and the failure of his great love for Mary Joyce, could only be consoled by communion with those scenes which, in his happy childhood, had nurtured his spiritual growth. The woods and fields around his cottage at Helpstone were not, in Clare's mind, of a different order of existence from his own. The things of nature were part of his own reality and existence, and his love for his surroundings was as intense as any human passion, and more permanent.

From boyhood he had been of a solitary disposition. He had befriended the gipsies, but was shunned by his fellow-villagers; he would walk the unenclosed common land, kicking his poems out of the clods, alone. "Solitude and God are one to me," he wrote. Yet he was no pantheist. The God he found in loneliness was a different being to the Deity he addressed in many of his unhappily mannered early sonnets. In religion, as in politics, Clare was content to stand aside, and not meddle in affairs which he did not fully understand, and of which he was instinctively suspicious. Clare's Christianity was the orthodoxy of a labourer. The God he found in solitude was the beginning of an awareness of that "something far more deeply interfused," which he never aspired to pursue further.

From his earliest to his last days Clare remained dedicated to the countryside of his birthplace:

> the very crow
> Croaks music in my native field.

Walking over Primrose Hill on one of his invariably short visits to London, Clare is said to have found a violet, the sight of which moved him so deeply that he immediately departed again for Helpstone, with which he associated the flower. The poem *The Flyting* commemorates a migration to a new house only three miles away, but nevertheless in an alien countryside for Clare. As a final example of Clare's extraordinary love for his birthplace (bred, understandably, from his minute and fond knowledge of it) may be quoted the solemn and tearful farewell that he paid certain elm-trees near his cottage, which were destined to be felled.

> And all old favourites, fond taste approves
> Griev'd me at heart to witness their removes.

There is, it should be added, in these last lines, a strong indication of the conservatism of Clare's nature, and his dislike of change. Although he had cause, he was never inclined to radicalism, and he deplored the protests and violence that men in his own circumstances were stirring up throughout the countryside. Nevertheless, Clare was strongly opposed to the enclosure of common land, and in *The Village Minstrel* he departed from his usual practice of ignoring political matters to inveigh against it.

> Inclosure, thou'art a curse upon the land.

In all matters such as this Clare's opinion may be taken as typical of the English labourer of the period, and it is an unexpected and ironical change, after reading the poetry of his more fortunate contemporaries, to learn that for Clare,

> Whate'er with time has sanction found,
> Is welcome, and is dear to me.

The accuracy of Clare's observation, which has already been stressed, might well be a mixed blessing to the poet. The example of the over-precise botanical sonnets of his contemporary, Charlotte Smith, is a warning of the perils that beset a purely photographic descriptive poet. Clare's observations are those of a naturalist, but they are more than that. "I love to look on nature with a poetic feeling, which magnifies the pleasure," he claimed, and although the accuracy of his observation has, on occasions, something of the factualism of White of Selborne—

> How curious is the nest; no other bird
> Uses such loose materials, or weaves
> Its dwelling in such spots: dead oaken leaves
> Are placed without, and velvet moss within,
> And little scraps of grass. . . .

more frequently the "poetic feeling" predominates. Clare's description of a snail in *Summer Images* is a magnificent example of minute observation transformed in a single line—the last—into pure and sensitive poetry:

> The jetty snail creeps from the mossy thorn,
> With earnest heed, and tremulous intent,
> Frail brother of the morn,
> That from the tiny bent's dew-misted leaves
> Withdraws his timid horn,
> And fearful vision weaves.

The gentleness and love that Clare everywhere exhibits in his poetry made physical violence and cruelty abhorrent to him. Lubin, in *The Village Minstrel*, a character as autobiographical as Bloomfield's Giles or Duck's thresher, is more an observer of the village sports and activities than a participant; but badger-baiting and cock-fighting were "sports too barbarous" to be even witnessed. The sight of a hay-maker who broke his back falling from a loaded waggon, Clare confessed, never ceased to haunt him. Such examples of poetic sensitivity are notable only in that they mark Clare as a figure who, despite his upbringing, had few emotional responses in common with his fellow-villagers. Even in that place that he knew and loved best, Helpstone, Clare was mentally isolated. "I live here among the ignorant like a lost man." His own mother, he says, "believed the higher parts of learning was the blackest arts of witchcraft." In consequence Clare, with his overwhelming capacity for love, was destined to be a man with few intimate friends.

The genius for poetry that made him happy gave him the reason for discontent; but the want and privation from which he and his family were seldom free did not intrude into Clare's verse. For him poetry was the remedy, not the symptom of misery. Nevertheless, for his own child he prays,

> But keep thee from my failings free,—
> Nor itch at rhymes.

In his boyhood Clare had experienced his only unalloyed happiness, and the girl he had loved from his youth he took as the symbol of all the loveliness he desired from the world. Mary Joyce was the daughter of a well-to-do farmer, and Clare, a field-labourer with no prospects, was not considered suitable company for the girl. They were little more than children when they parted, but Mary's image remained with Clare throughout his life. Indeed, as his madness grew upon him she became more real than his wife, Patty. It was not without reason that Clare, in his asylum, claimed to have two wives; for Mary was as firmly wedded to him in the spirit as Patty was in the flesh. Five years before he was certified as insane Mary conversed with Clare in his dreams, and appeared before him in his imagination. It was to return to Mary, not Patty and his children, that Clare escaped from the Epping asylum and walked eighty miles home. "She is my good genius and I believe in her ideally almost as fresh as reality," he declared.

Clare's published works contain a number of poems addressed both to Mary and to Patty. His autobiographical manner of recording daily scenes and incidents made this quite natural. To both girls he dedicated unaffected and charming love-lyrics, and every country lass appearing in his "landscapes with figures" may be said to have been modelled on one or other of them. Clare never delineates his figures with as much detail as he bestows on the natural objects that surround them; one ploughboy is very similar to another, one lover to the next; so the reader cannot obtain much impression of the character of either of Clare's loves from the poems alone. As the years passed, Mary became the unrivalled object of his poetic affections. It is she whom he watched milking, or nutting, or at the village fair; and Clare will at times abandon his make-believe dalliance to apostrophize with real pathos,

> O Mary, can'st thou feel the past
> And keep thy heart unbroken?

As madness closed in around him Mary and the world of external nature remained the only stable things in the struggle to establish his identity in which he became engaged.

> I am: yet what I am none cares or knows,
> My friends forsake me like a memory lost,
> I am the self-consumer of my woes—
> They rise and vanish in oblivious host,

he wrote in his most famous poem. The injustice of his fate, his family and friends, even his reputation as a poet, came to have no place in his mind, which was all-absorbed in love of the countryside, and of his ideal of womanhood. A similar, but more tempestuous, ecstasy produced *Jubilate Agno* from Christopher Smart. The love-lyrics Clare wrote in the asylum transcend any of his published verses. He seems to have achieved freedom of expression, and to have broken his fetters of loam. He addresses his imaginary love (Mary Joyce herself was many years dead) with a warmth of enthusiasm, and dramatic intensity, of which he was incapable before. In his greatest long poem, *Child Harold*, written under his Byronic delusion, he tells of the agony of his love for Mary, a love which, he feels, excuses a wasted life.

> Mary, thy name loved long still keeps me free,
> Till my lost life becomes a part of thee.

In the last years of his life the name itself vanishes, and Mary appears in many guises. At times she mingles with his second great enthusiasm, the world of nature, and "Helen" becomes associated with the seasonal change. In the winter season, and in the winter of his life, Clare expects her to return to him with the spring.

> I still expected Helen
> Would blossom with the spring.

Taking into account such influences on the poetical career of John Clare as the poverty which even the short-lived success of his poems did little to relieve, the hopelessness with which he viewed his increasing liabilities, and his inability to earn by labouring, or by writing, sufficient on which to support his family; and setting against this burden of care his understanding and adoration of the objects of external nature in his immediate neighbourhood, and his deep love for the Galatea his imagination had built up from the memory of Mary Joyce, we may now approach chronologically, and in more detail, the body of Clare's poetry.

Clare began to write poetry early in his life, principally inspired, he tells us, by finding in *The Seasons* a record of such beauties as he himself was familiar with, made new and wonderful under the poetic vision. In his publisher's words, "It called forth all the passion of his soul for poetry," and in his own, "the opening lines of Spring . . . made my heart twitter with joy."

Although it was *The Seasons* that first inspired Clare to write, the earliest of his poems, composed in imitation of Thomson's manner, have no great merit. The majority of them were burnt in ignorance by his mother, for Clare was ashamed to admit to poetical pretensions. The earliest that is preserved, *The Fate of Amy*, written at the age of fourteen, was included in his first published volume, *Poems Descriptive of Rural Life and Scenery*. After Clare's name on the title-page was added, "A Northamptonshire Peasant." The introduction, in which his publisher, John Taylor, brought his protégé to the notice of the public, attempts primarily to justify Clare as a poet in his own right, but failing this, Taylor appeals to the indulgence, and in the last paragraph even to the charity, of the reader.

The following Poems will probably attract some notice by their intrinsic merit; but they are also entitled to attention from the circumstances under which they are written. . . . No Poet of our Country has shewn greater ability, under circumstances so hostile to its developement.

Taylor's appeal for charity was not written without cause. Clare had never been able to obtain permanent work; the agricultural depression and his own physical weakness had made casual and uncongenial labour his only means of supporting not only himself but his crippled parents, and Patty, his future wife, who was bearing him a child. By turns Clare had worked as gardener, soldier, and lime-burner; the publication of his poems, and the resulting patronage that was bestowed upon him, resulted in a small fixed income of just over £40 a year. This amount was little enough. Even Bloomfield, with far fewer responsibilities, was not so poor. Added to this the activities of a poet made it increasingly difficult for him to obtain field-labour. The publication of his poems, therefore, although it seemed to relieve him of all financial worries, did little but postpone them for a few years.

The poems in Clare's first volume are an interesting medley of songs, ballads, descriptive pieces, and sonnets. They have, however, a uniformity of texture, caused largely by Clare's imitation of Augustan models, and his severely limited vocabulary. So scanty an education, and so haphazard and unselective an acquaintance with books, must of necessity be reflected in a poet's early verse. Although enthusiasm for his natural surroundings is apparent, Clare seldom touches the heart. He views the scene with some detachment, and to gain fluency he unconsciously becomes trite.

The use of provincialisms Clare, quite rightly, defended; and in a letter to Taylor, he justified such phrases as "Eggs on" and "Twit-a-twit." "I heartily desire no word of mine to be altered," he declared, ". . . for it is the Language of Nature, and that can never be disgusting." Many of the dialect words, and especially the verbs which Clare uses, are undeniably powerful. Burns and Barnes, who also used the unrefined language of countrymen, would have endorsed Clare's own judgment that "putting the correct Language of the Gentleman into the mouth of a Simple Shepherd or Vulgar Ploughman is far from Natural." And it was naturalism above all things for which Clare strove. There is an artlessness in such lines as,

> When tootling robins carol-welcomes sing,
> And sparrows chelp glad tidings from the eaves,

that a direct statement could only make prosaic.

Despite the awkward addition of a four-page glossary at the back of the book, Clare's dialect verbs undoubtedly add considerable vividness and beauty to poems that are otherwise baldly factual. Owls "mope out," men "soddle home," and "the sleepy rustic sloomy goes." But Clare is not primarily a dialect poet, and at his best, as in *Evening*, he achieves a happy description with the simplest and most unaffected of vocabularies.

> Now buzzing, with unwelcome din,
> The heedless beetle bangs
> Against the cow-boy's dinner tin,
> That o'er his shoulder hangs.

Against such felicities must be set the frequent padding for the sake of the rhyme, and the misuse of Augustan phraseology. The lines *To the Glow-Worm*, which commence "Tasteful Illumination of the night,"

or, in *Helpstone*, the circumlocution, "the shepherd's woolly charge,"
are unfortunate debts to Thomson, and so is the use of abstract nouns
in *Approach of Spring*, "But still Hope's smiles unpoint the thorns
of Care." Faults such as these Clare soon learnt not to repeat; neither
did he continue (except in such lunatic verses as *Don Juan*) to express
sentiments that offended his principal patron, and well-meaning friend,
Lord Radstock. Lines such as

> Accursed Wealth! o'er bounding human laws,
> Of every evil thou remain'st the cause,
> Victims of want, those wretches such as me,
> Too truly lay their wretchedness to thee,

in *Helpstone*, or

> Feed the hungry, ere they die,
> Think, oh! think upon the poor,
> Nor against them shut thy door,

in an *Address to Plenty* were hardly likely to be received with
favour. But although such thoughts can never have been far absent
from Clare's mind, in his poetry he was usually unwilling to express
them. Cobbett's radicalism received only his tepid support; like
Bloomfield he was not a reformer at heart, as his own ambitions
indicate. In a poetic reverie he describes his ideal life should
fortune favour him. It is lowly enough in conception: a warm,
thatched cottage, with books and an easy chair, food and drink, and—
a significant addition—freedom from debt.

Lord Radstock had also objected to the coarseness of certain of
Clare's poems, and this element, though utterly suppressed in the
works published during his lifetime, can be detected again in certain
of the less ordered asylum verses. The poem to which Lord Radstock
took particular exception was in imitation of Cowper, and entitled
My Mary. Clare, whilst stressing his fidelity to his own Mary,
catalogues her faults and failings without glozing.

> For though in stature mighty small,
> And near as thick as thou art tall,
> The hand made thee, that made us all,
>   My Mary.

It is heavy-handed humour: Barnes is infinitely subtler on a subject of this nature. But either Lord Radstock's protest, or Clare's own sensibility, scotched any similar effusions.

The youth and felicity of so much of his early verse owe much to Cunningham, from whom Clare learnt to use a variety of stanzaic forms. Duck and Bloomfield seldom ventured beyond the heroic couplet, but Clare was never afraid to experiment. The sonnets which he composed are perhaps the least satisfactory; indeed they have little but the fourteen lines in common with traditional models. It is probable that Clare did not fully understand the purpose of such poems, as he tends to use them for conveniently short descriptive passages, occasionally adding a hastily improvised moral.

Clare's deep love for all living things (and it is from where his affections lie that his truest poetry originates) can be frequently detected in this early volume. "A sparrow's life's as sweet as ours," he says in *Summer Evening* and the same sentiment recurs in *On a Lost Greyhound*,

> For dogs, as men, are equally
> A link in Nature's chain.

Birds, beasts, "tiny, nameless things," even *An Insignificant Flower*, which, like Wordsworth, Clare will stoop to notice, are as dear to the poet as are his fellow human beings. But unlike Wordsworth's, Clare's love was not a means towards a profounder end; he shared with Keats a dislike of poetry that had a palpable design upon the reader. Clare merely considered himself on a parity with the creations of nature. Himself a creature of the fields and woods, he acknowledged himself to be a link in the natural chain, joined, but not superior, to a dog or a sparrow.

It is always sad, when one contemplates all the happiness that Clare found in the world around him, to realize how little the poet was to experience in his own life. Particularly tragic are the two youthful desires that he expressed, both of which he was to be denied. In his poem *A Reflection in Autumn*, Clare, watching the leaves fall from a tree, saw a similitude in his own dissolution.

> Just so 'twill fare with me in Autumn's Life;
> Just so I'd wish: but may the trunk and all
> Die with the leaves.

For nearly thirty years the trunk of Clare's body was destined to live after his leaves had fallen. Even then his second wish, voiced in *Help-stone*, might have been granted.

> And, as reward for all my troubles past,
> Find one hope true—to die at home at last.

But it was in an asylum, far from his birthplace, that, in 1864, he died.

Thomas Sheridan is reported to have said, "wonder usually accompanied by a bad taste, looks only for what is uncommon; and if a work comes out under the name of a thresher, a bricklayer, a milk-woman, or—a lord, it is sure to be eagerly sought after by the million." Clare's first volume certainly produced a gratifying amount of notice, and a number of the influential reviews devoted space to his poems. The most important of these, and the most searching in its critical assessment of Clare's genius, was written by Gilchrist in *The Quarterly Review*. "Examples of minds, highly gifted by nature," he wrote, "struggling with and breaking through the bondage of adversity, are not rare in this country; but privation is not destitution."

The New Monthly considered that Clare had imitated Burns too freely, and many reviewers cautioned him not to desert his manual labour on the strength of ephemeral fame; but there was no adverse comment, and the majority of the notices were enthusiastic. *The Eclectic Review* found "extraordinary merit" in the poems, *The Anti-Jacobin Review* considered them the "production of a second Burns," and for several weeks *The Morning Post* printed letters and news items about the peasant-poet.

The effect of such support and encouragement made Clare hasten to produce a second volume of poems, based on a series of village stories. Taylor, who had suggested this subject, obviously had the popularity of Crabbe in mind, and hoped that, should he be able to impart human interest to his poems, Clare might rival his fellow East Anglian in popularity. "Action is what I want I am told," Clare wrote in his diary. But the action in these village stories lacked spirit and fire, and Taylor, who acted as Clare's editor, correcting spelling, grammar and sentiment as he thought fit, abandoned the idea.

Some of the sixteen tales were printed in *The Village Minstrel*, Clare's second collection of poems, which appeared in 1821 in two volumes. Although the general standard of poetry in this book was higher, it was not so popular as *Poems Descriptive*. The reviewers, however, continued to be complimentary, and the book sold tolerably well. The poem from which the book takes its title was the most ambitious that Clare had attempted; written in Spenserian stanzas, it was autobiographical in subject—somewhat similar to the work of Duck and Bloomfield in its record of the cycle of life on the land. But whereas the earlier poets were primarily concerned with the daily round of the day-labourer, Clare's Lubin, with the disposition of a dreamer and a solitary, wanders alone, "and he could tell how the shy squirrel far'd." Clare is never at his best in a sustained poem, and although occasional phrases and sentiments have the stamp of pure poetry, much is prosaic.

Throughout the verses there is a nostalgic melancholy; Clare is constantly recollecting his childhood days, when he visited the gipsies who camped on the unenclosed common land, or watched the harvest-home, or village wakes. And above all things, Clare endows Lubin with his own unalterable affection for his cottage home.

In literature, as in art, the landscape is perhaps the most difficult of visual forms to reproduce without flatness or distortion. This is particularly true of the low-lying East Anglian fens. But even such unprepossessing countrysides have their admirers. Crome and De Wint delighted in painting it, and Crabbe, on the East Coast, described it in verse. To such a small band of enthusiasts Clare belonged, yet no artist or poet could rival him in the closeness of his observation, or the parochialism of his affections. The countryside around Peterborough has little that would arrest attention, and it is therefore all the more surprising to find how much beauty Clare can discover amongst

> Swamps of wild rush-beds, and slough's squashy traces,
> Grounds of rough fallows with thistle and weed.

One of the most impressive poems in *The Village Minstrel* is *Autumn*, a subject that immediately invites comparison with Keats's ode on that subject. In perception and design Clare's poem rivals Keats's, but Clare lacks the imagination and selectivity of subject-matter that makes Keats's ode so much the superior. Clare's pastoral is a lifelike recording of birds silent in the trees, boys nutting, "and grunting noise of rambling hogs," the labourers threshing and hedging, and the robin that "dithering droops his ruffled wing." There is all the bustle and activity of a Breughel painting. A small, but interesting, comparison presents itself in this poem, between Pope's and Clare's description of a hunter shooting a pheasant. The graceful, tapestry-like incident in *Windsor Forest* is a strange contrast to the minute realism (aided by one of Clare's powerful coined verbs) of

> A certain aim the gunner takes,
> He clumsy fluskers up, and falls.

Although lack of selectivity may be considered a flaw in *Autumn*, it has a delightful effect in a less ambitious poem such as *Recollections after a Ramble*. Here, in a guided walk around the fields of Helpstone, Clare points out how, after a shower, bees cling to the flowers, unable to fly, or observes the "milk-white bellies" of fish playing in a pool.

In *The Village Minstrel* is Clare's first pastoral poem written consciously as a modern adaptation of a classical form. Of this poem, *William and Robin*, Taylor wrote to Clare saying that Keats "likes your first pastoral . . . very much indeed." Clare and Keats never met, but having the same publisher, they had read something of each other's poetry. Keats's remark, after reading Clare's *Solitude*, that description prevailed too much over the sentiment, contains some, but by no means all, of the truth. When one considers how little success uneducated poets have achieved when they have exchanged naturalism for sentiment, and courted the Muse instead of recording nature, one is thankful that Clare was stubborn and rejected all such advice. On a point of poetic criticism Keats was right, but from the point of view of poetic expediency he was wrong. Clare's opinion of *Endymion*, it is interesting to notice, is almost the same criticism reversed.

The frequency of . . . classical accomplishments makes it wearisome to the reader, . . . in spite of all this his descriptions of scenery are often very fine . . . But . . . he often described Nature as she appeared to his fancies, and not as he would have described her had he witnessed the things he described,

Six years elapsed before Clare's third book was published. His editor, Taylor, had many other interests, and *The Shepherd's Calendar* was delayed until all popular interest in Clare's poetry had waned. A new poetry-reading public was evolving. The aristocratic tradition of patronage was virtually dead, and the middle classes, who, in the second half of the century, took Tennyson and Browning to their hearts, had not yet come into their own. The 'twenties and 'thirties were lean years for the majority of poets, and a number of publishers who did not realize this trend went out of business.

Meanwhile Clare's financial position was becoming more and more precarious. On Taylor's recommendation he wrote for the reviews, and for the annuals, but payments were small, and often could not be collected. *The Shepherd's Calendar* does, however, mark an advance in Clare's poetic genius. His vocabulary had widened, and his choice of words was more selective and accurate. His subject-matter does not vary, but it is astonishing how seldom he repeats himself. He seems to have copied from nature herself an infinite variety of scenes, but he has not so great a range of moods. There is an evenness of temper and an emotional control that tends to deaden the sparkle and spontaneity of which we know he was capable. The editorial pen of Taylor may have been partly responsible, but, whatever the cause, it was not until his asylum years that his singing was completely unconstrained.

The name poem of *The Shepherd's Calendar* is descriptive. A poem is written for each month, in a variety of metrical forms. As might be expected, it owes much to *The Seasons*, but it is more closely factual, swifter in movement, and lacking in the sentimental anecdotes of Thomson's poem. But Clare's literary debts (which are frequent and apparent in much of his poetry) are taken from a wider range of reading. An echo from the opening of *Hyperion* in *June*,

> And in the oven-heated air,
> Not one light thing is floating there,

and from *L'Allegro* in *September*.

> While Mirth, that at the scene abides,
> Laughs, till she almost cracks her sides,

are only two examples amongst many. It is not to be wondered at, nor should it be held against him, that a poet as receptive as Clare, who was learning and creating at the same time, should be more than usually prone to incorporate phrases and paraphrases from sources that he admired. The lack of any continuity in so long a bucolic poem is a disadvantage, and *The Shepherd's Calendar* has not even a central figure like Giles or Lubin to carry the action forward from month to month. Nevertheless, for all its faults, it is a poem of considerable merit, and a consolidation, if not an actual advance, in Clare's poetic achievement. The shorter poems with which the book ends contain lyrics, some village stories, and sonnets; the latter are, as usual, for the most part clumsy.

Clare's last published work, *The Rural Muse*, brought him little money, and less praise. Erroneously, it was considered that Clare was well off compared to Bloomfield and Burns. Readers of feeling, who were interested in purely descriptive poetry, had become increasingly few. Even Bowles was losing favour. Clare was adjured to describe the manners and feelings of the lower orders, but even if such advice had been profitable, it came too late. Already there were signs of Clare's mental derangement, which had been stimulated by his removal to a cottage some three miles from Helpstone. He could no longer concentrate on poems of any length, but his lyrical verses reached, during these years, a high standard of excellence. John Wilson, almost alone among the reviewers, recognized Clare's increasing powers, and praised the poems generously.

The poet in Clare reaches a felicity which the recorder of nature could never achieve. It is poems such as *Summer Images* that justify Mr. Edmund Blunden's uncompromising statement that "John Clare [is] in some lights the best poet of Nature that this country and for all I know any other country ever produced."

> I love at early morn, from new mown swath,
> To see the startled frog his route pursue;
> To mark while, leaping o'er the dripping path,
> His bright sides scatter dew.

On occasions Clare seems to rise to a courageous, almost defiant, realization of his position as an inspired poet, with all the anguish and elation that such a dedication entails,

> True Poesy owns a haunted mind,
> A thirst-enduring flame,
> Burning the soul to leave behind
> The memory of a name.

There are here the first traces of the heroic *blague* that was to thread its way through the asylum verses in scribbled abuse against Queen Victoria, boastings of being a superior poet to Byron, and finally to achieve greatness in *A Vision*:

> I snatch'd the sun's eternal ray
> And wrote till earth was but a name.

Whilst much of *The Rural Muse* is poetry of great distinction, there is an inevitable proportion of indifferent verse. Clare was seldom really bad. The level of his poetry is surprisingly high; but he did not achieve any commendable results when he celebrated such figures as Charles Lamb, Napoleon, or Izaak Walton, or addressed Boston church, in a Bowlesian manner, as "Majestic pile!" Clare's poetry, like his life, was inextricably linked with his home fields.

In 1837, at the instigation of Taylor, Clare was admitted to Dr. Allen's private asylum at High Beech, near Epping, where for four years he grew healthy and burly of body, but fretful of mind. During his time there, and (after his long walk home) in the Northamptonshire County Asylum, where he was committed as insane "after years addicted to poetical prosings," he wrote spasmodically a number of poems, some bearing distinct traces of mental derangement, but the majority of a direct and pure simplicity, with much of the freshness of an early world upon them. Clare's insanity, like that of Kit Smart, was not noxious to society, but to be confined even in a well-administered institution never ceased to make Clare unhappy. "Literature has destroyed my head and brought me here," he declared.

When the poetic spirit moved him he seemed to forget his brooding melancholy, and, for the most part, his extravagant delusions. He wrote fast, and would never correct a poem once it was written, nor would he complete any verses at which he had been disturbed. No longer was poetry a conscious process of composition, but he used it as an instrument whereby he could search in the past for retrospective happiness. In the quest for identity, which his madness stimulated, poetry aided lucidity. For the first time in his life Clare was free from the troubles and anxieties of the world. He could recollect in tranquillity all that he remembered of the emotions of his youth.

> The woods and fields were all the books I knew,
> And every leisure thought was Love and Fame.

Clare was now content to acknowledge that "My life hath been a wreck," but that no longer worried him. All his thoughts were directed towards the mental tranquillity that he most desired.

> Oh, for that sweet, untroubled rest
> That poets oft have sung!—
> The babe upon its mother's breast,
> The bird upon its young,
> The heart asleep without a pain—
> When shall I know that sleep again?

In his old age Clare seems to capture the visionary gleam, and enter into a child's world, with all its grave and simple wonder. In all his poems Clare had looked back to his boyhood in Helpstone; in these last verses he was back, and seeing, as if for the first time, all the innocence and beauty of the world around him.

> Little trotty wagtail, he went in the rain
> And tittering tottering sideways, he near got straight again,
> He stooped to get a worm, and look'd up to catch a fly,
> And then he flew away ere his feathers they were dry.

The ladybird, concealed in a cowslip-bell, talked to him.

> In the cowslip pips I lie
> Hidden from the buzzing fly,
> Where green grass beneath me lies
> Pearled wi' dew like fishes' eyes.
> Here I lie, a clock-a-clay,
> Waiting for the time o' day.

But Clare was not wholly preoccupied with childhood. As we have seen, his love for Mary Joyce found its most passionate expression in these asylum poems, and his observation of natural objects (for he had considerable liberty to roam in the grounds of the asylum) was as acute as ever. In the dusk he sees

> the owl on wheaten wing,
> And white hood scowling o'er his eyes.

In the last poem he ever wrote, when he was nearly seventy years old, he watched a chaffinch building its nest.

It would seem that a recollected line from some familiar poem would often inspire verses of his own. A number of these asylum fragments begin with such lines as, "I love the blue violet that creeps on the mossy bank," "She walks in beauty and in light," or "Ladybird, Ladybird! Where art thou gone?" The superior merit of these poems from the asylum over those earlier ones that Clare published has often been exaggerated, but it is undeniable that the imaginative quality that should irradiate a record of fact and observation only flickers through the early poems. During the long years in the asylum, when Clare no longer cared about poetry, but was more concerned about his reputation as a prize-fighter, the union of those two same qualities was unconsciously effected.

In so short a space one cannot hope to do justice to the poetic genius of John Clare, but in recent years the obscurity that clouded his name for a half-century after his death has largely been dissipated, and his life and works have been fittingly memorialized. But perhaps the greatest enigma remains, and will remain, unresolved: how the seeds of poetry came to germinate in such ill-prepared ground.

A Wordsworthian explanation might be that Clare's only distinction from a host of his fellow-labourers was an ability to express himself.

> Many are the Poets that are sown
> By Nature; men endowed with highest gifts,
> The vision and the faculty divine;
> Yet wanting the accomplishment of verse,

—a theory that has been strongly refuted by both Goethe and Swinburne. In their opinion a mute, inglorious Milton is a contradiction in terms. "There is no such thing as a dumb poet or a handless painter," declared Swinburne. "The essence of an artist is that he should be articulate." Whichever view one inclines towards it necessarily focuses particular attention on those first impulses that either fashion or awake the latent spirit of creation, especially in men whose station in life seemed otherwise far removed from the realms of poetry. How often this has been caused by the reading of a single poem. John Taylor, the Elizabethan waterman, acknowledged it to be *Hero and Leander*. In the case of Stephen Duck it was Milton who was his inspiration; but both Bloomfield and Clare wrote poetry after having read *The Seasons*.

All these poets (with the possible exception of Taylor) were abnormally sensitive to the emotional effects of verse. Duck would tremble on hearing Shakespeare read aloud, and De Quincey reports that Clare became more than usually animated when Wordsworth was spoken of. But although poetry became an impelling force, it was usually one that deprived them of happiness in their lives. Taylor, hardly an inspired poet, and better adapted to withstand the buffets of life than men of greater sensitivity, reflected that poetry

> Proved to me a blessing and a curse,
> To fill my pate with verse, and empt my purse.

Taylor accustomed himself to living by his wits, and was an opportunist in verse. Duck, too, with his regular employment followed by secure patronage, led a less poetically-oppressed life than Bloomfield or Clare. Only in Clare's case did poetry not just occupy a part of life but dominate it emotionally. Duck and Bloomfield all too readily forgot the scenes of their childhood and youth. The poetry they wrote when young enthusiasms swept them quickly deteriorated into occasional verse.

It was Clare, however, whose instinct for what was the true subject of his poetry, and whose refusal to be diverted by his more sophisticated friends from an unambitious, but perfectible, method of expression, who withstood the hitherto inevitably contaminating touch of society.

In a poem *To the Memory of Bloomfield*, he asserted that

> The tide of fashion is a stream too strong
> For pastoral brooks, that gently flow and sing.

Although he realized Bloomfield's essential failings, Clare was among his greatest admirers. He contemplated writing his biography, and they exchanged letters and books, but never met. It was undoubtedly through the success of Bloomfield's poems that Clare, an incomparably better poet, achieved his short-lived fame.

The fact that the two poets rose from such similar circumstances made comparisons inevitable. Gilchrist, whose review of *Poems Descriptive* did so much to establish Clare's reputation, who later became a firm friend, and who introduced the poet to a sympathetic and illustrious circle of literary figures in London, was quick to point out that Clare's poems were of superior merit, and the circumstances under which they were written less favourable, than Bloomfield's or Burns's. "*The Farmer's Boy*," Gilchrist remarked,

is the result of careful observations made on the occupations and habits, with few references to the passions of rural life. Clare writes frequently from the same suggestions, but his subject is always enlivened by picturesque and minute description of the landscape around him, and deepened, as we have said, with a powerful reference to emotions within. The one is descriptive, the other contemplative.

Clare was fortunate in having such poets as Wordsworth, Coleridge, Thomson, and Burns, all of whom he admired, to learn from, if not to emulate. For him it was not necessary to take Lamb's advice and model his style on Shenstone's. But his eighteenth-century predecessors had access only to the mannered verse of contemporary poets, who, for the most part, took little delight in external nature.

> Green fields, and shady groves, and chrystal springs,
> And larks, and nightingales, are odious things,

declared Young. Clare was probably more of a child of romanticism than is generally recognized, writing as nature, and not as man, directed. The quality of his poetry is the vindication of his choice.

> I gave my name immortal birth,
> And kept my spirit with the free.

The Language of Speech:
Relph and Barnes

Nature hath made one World, and Art another. In brief, all things are artificial; for Nature is the Art of GOD.

SIR THOMAS BROWNE: *Religio Medici*

Except in the very earliest days of the language the various English dialects have seldom been used in poetry. The Scots have always been proud to reproduce in the more permanent written form the distinctive features of their spoken words, and the Welsh have made use of their own language; but in England there has always been a shyness over departing from the accepted standards of Queen's English. Vernacular expression in various parts of the country is highly distinctive and original; the natural speech of the majority of the poets that have been considered in these pages must have possessed many inflections, idioms, and turns of phrase that were peculiar to their area. Duck, we have heard, had "a mixture of the Rustick" in his speech, and Clare must have been noticeable at Taylor's literary dinners for his slow, East Anglian way of talking. Although such characteristics were never entirely lost in the speech of these men, it was a prime qualification that their writing should be smoothed, pruned and rendered palatable to a refined taste by the removal of all dialectal eccentricities. Rightly or wrongly it was considered by patrons and booksellers alike that the public would not tolerate any deviation from the linguistic norm. The only occasions when provincial forms could be safely used was in a humorous context, and generally speaking that opinion holds good today.

For a peasant-poet the local dialect would seem an ideal method of communication. There would be no need for him to strive for an elevated style, or to ape literary manners to which he was unaccustomed.

If critics had been prepared to believe that, on certain occasions, the language of common speech could be used as the language of poetry, there would, doubtless, have been more and better poetry written by artisans and labourers. But the hostility Wordsworth met at the end of the eighteenth century in propounding such a doctrine (which he never himself quite followed) is sufficient indication why the majority of poets in the circumstances of Duck or Bloomfield attempted the double labour of achieving gentility as well as poetic expression.

The advantages of uneducated poets writing dialect poetry are obvious. Sincerity would be gained and directness of expression achieved. It would not have been necessary for such poets to have had before them models whose technique alone would have heightened their innate sense of inferiority; Milton as an inspiration was a very different matter from Milton as a guide to composition. The intellectual equipment of an uneducated man is usually confined to instinctive or deductive reasoning within the narrow field of what is familiar to him. A dialect poet need never stray from these confines; the language he uses would not take him farther.

The weaknesses of the dialect as a poetic cloak must not be overlooked. A great deal of bad verse can be given a superficial relish by the strangeness of dialectal form. There is also a danger that the beauty, rhythm, and even the meaning may be lost to the reader unfamiliar with the transliterated sounds and speech-forms of the particular vernacular. Obscurity, especially in the simple utterances of peasants, is certainly to be avoided. A tendency is also observable in Relph's, though not in Barnes's, poetry to lose all trace of dignity when using the dialect. This self-conscious habit is natural enough, though unfortunate, in an age when Somerville's *Hobbinol* and Gay's pastorals reflected the fashion for derision when writing about rural pursuits.

Dialect words add richness and texture to the language, but they need to be used discreetly and always in their topographical context. Relph and Barnes never strayed far from Sebergham and the Vale of Blackmore, so they were never tempted to furbish up their Muses. In addition neither of them thought their poetry sufficiently important to bother about public opinion or public taste. They both wrote without thought of gain or fame, and although neither of them was a peasant, both of them, by vitue of their pastoral duties, sympathized with and understood the flocks over which they were vicars.

Many poorly-born poets, such as Duck and Crabbe, were eventually trained for ordination. The Church offered an easy and inconspicuous niche for those of whom society thought well but did not wish to support—a belated adaptation of the mediaeval system whereby the monks took in and trained the most promising youths from poor families in the neighbourhood. But Barnes and Relph were clergymen and teachers first and foremost, and only because they knew their parishioners so well through daily contact, and were simple, unassuming men, do they in any way qualify to be considered in a study of peasant poetry. Their birth and station certainly did not take "the way that takes the town," they were true poets of the countryside in this respect—unlike the socialite Thomson—and although they had been betrayed to a lingering book, they were never as divorced from practical matters as was Duck amongst the waxworks in Merlin's Cave. Barnes, and probably Relph before him, could wield a scythe, and knew the intricacies of agriculture as well as his neighbours.

Josiah Relph was born at Sebergham, a small village in the northern foothills of the Cumberland fells, where they begin to flatten out before the plains around Carlisle. Until he was fifteen he was educated at Appleby, some twenty-five miles away in Westmorland. From there he was sent to Glasgow University; but he never completed his course, and returned to Sebergham to act as a master at the Grammar School, with a salary dependent on voluntary subscription. In this lowly and unprofitable position he remained, writing a little poetry when he had time, and translating the classics, but never seeking favour or preferment for himself.

When the minister died Relph succeeded to his place. It was no great advancement. The parish of Sebergham was a perpetual curacy with a stipend of £30 a year—a sum well beneath that which made the clergyman at Auburn "passing rich." Relph seems to have been perfectly content to spend his life in this isolated and wild corner of Britain, without hope or desire to move elsewhere, and to receive a labourer's wage. Even this was not granted him for long; he died in his thirty-second year in 1743. Four years later a volume of his poems was published in Glasgow by subscription. Amongst those who received copies were Stephen Duck and his third wife.

With a fatalistic anticipation of the failure of Relph's poems to achieve even a passing fame, the preface is almost an apology. "We cannot indeed recommend these Poems as any standard of polite taste and elevated genius, nor as perfect patterns for imitation." In the middle of the eighteenth century such poetry as Relph's needed an excuse. To write in the dialect, and to write unsatirically of low subjects were faults indeed. The *Proeme* to Gay's pastorals would have given Relph a precedent, had not Gay had a satirical purpose— to deride the spate of imitative verse that followed the publication of Pope's pastorals in 1709—as his real object in writing such poems. To read *The Shepherd's Week* blind to its ironical content is as near a parallel to the poetry of Relph as the half-century affords. "Thou wilt not find my shepherdesses idly piping on oaten reeds," declared Gay,

but milking the kine, tying up the sheaves, or if the hogs are astray driving them to their styes. My shepherd gathereth none other nosegays but what are the growth of our own fields, he sleepeth not under myrtle shades, but under a hedge, nor does he vigilantly defend his flocks from wolves, because there are none.

Gay was too volatile and town-bred a wit to really understand the rural scene. What he thought ludicrous, Theocritus in modern dress, Relph produced seriously, not to refute the Golden Age, but to record Cumberland in verse.

Relph's most successful verses are those in which he combines the vernacular with the pastoral convention; but the dialect monologue that he was so fond of using is truer to the nature of the speaker than to the bucolic tradition. In *Harvest, or the Bashful Shepherd*, a time-worn subject, the bashful swain who cannot express his love is treated in a very new way. Robin and Betty are the protagonists, not Corydon and Phillida, and at the first sight of his lady-love Robin quite un-romantically cuts himself with his sickle. His face, he says, was even redder than his injured hand.

146

> Away I sleeng'd, to Grandy meade my mean
> My Grandy (God be wud her, now she's geane)
> Skilfu' the gushen bluid wi' cockwebs staid.

As his grandmother very well knew, cobwebs are an astringent; but although she could successfully cure Robin's cut, "My Grandy cou'd not cure a bleedin heart." For three years, he tells us, he has been in this state of moping indecision, too shy to approach the unwitting Betty, but too much in love to transfer his affections elsewhere. The solution that he eventually proposes is certainly a new departure from pastoral tradition.

> A buik theer is—a buik—the neame—shem faw't:
> Some thing o' compliments I think they caw't:
> 'At meakes a clownish lad a clever spark,
> O hed I this! this buik wa'd de my wark;
> And I's resolved to hav'et what ever't cost.

To implement his decision Robin is prepared to sell his flute and go off to Carlisle fair to purchase this desirable commodity, in order to be able on his return to write a "handsome letter" to the beloved he is too shy to approach.

Another dialect pastoral, this time in the form of a dialogue between two lovers, is called *Hay-time, or the Constant Lovers*. The pair, Cursty and Peggy, are raking the hay, and while it is drying they sit down and "their artless tale of love began." At first they are obviously more concerned with their work than with their emotions. One expects a love-duet, but is surprised to hear Cursty open the discussion in this manner:

> A finer hay-day seer was never seen;
> The greenish sops already luik less green;
> As weel the greenish sops will suin be dry'd
> As Sawney's bacco spred by th' ingle side.

This indeed is the language of common speech. The repetitiveness, the word-order, and the private, parochial simile give local colour to the lines; the dialect "sops" is a strong and thoroughly honest word to use, and helps bring the scene to life without being pretentious.

Both Cursty and Peggy agree that their life is a pleasant one, and

147

they do not envy their friends who are off to town, dressed in their Sunday clothes. In their conversation together they recollect the days of their childhood in pleasant (if somewhat limping) lines. Relph was never the craftsman of verse that Barnes was. Sometimes the dialect masked defects rather than added to poetic splendour. But in general these local pastorals of Relph's have a homely charm and are written in a chattily easy manner.

> Can thou remember, I remember't weel,
> Sin call wee things we claver'd owr yon steel;
> Lang willy-wands for hoops I yust to bay,
> To meake my canny lass a leady gay.

From their childhood Cursty and Peggy had been together, first as companions, now as lovers. Their recollections of the maturing of this love form the basis of the poem. Occasionally Relph achieves a splendid descriptive line ("See! owr the field the whurlin sunshine whiews"), but equally frequent are several very arch similitudes. "Sweet is this kiss as smell of dwallowed hay" is a laboured rusticism that inevitably reminds one of the consciously-conceived bathos of Gay's sardonic pastoral infelicities.

> Ah *Blouzelind*! I love thee more by half,
> Than does their fawns, or cows the new fall'n calf.

The sincerity of Relph's dialect poems is all the more apparent when one examines the rest of his productions, which are as bad as Augustan occasional verse can be. He seemed to need, even as the Lakers after him needed, the anchor of a known and familiar landscape. When he translated Theocritus and Horace into Cumberland Relph tried not only to adapt them to, but absorb them into, his parochial environs. Non-indigenous mythology, therefore, had to be ascribed to the only source by which it might be familiar to the Lakeland peasant.

> Thus Harculus, 'at (ballats say)
> Made parlish monsters stoop,
> Flang his great mikle club away,
> And tuik a spinnel up.

Relph's poem *St. Agnes Fast, or the Amorous Maiden,* is worth pausing over, if only because of the similarity of subject to Keats's great poem. It is an amusing account, in broad dialect, of all that passes through the mind of a young girl who is waiting and fasting on the Eve of St. Agnes in the hope that her lover, Roger, will make his appearance. It is a far less tranquil vigil than that of Keats's Madeline. Roger's girl is blessed with less patience and a great deal more frailty than Porphyro's. She is certainly not prepared to

> couch supine her beauties, lily white;
> Nor look behind, nor sideways, but require
> Of Heaven with upward eyes for all that she desires.

To start off with she is hungry.

> How lang I've fasted and 'tis hardly four;
> This day I doubt 'ill neer be gitten owr.

Thoroughly exasperated she goes on to recount all the superstitions and devices of which she has made use in order to be sure of ensnaring Roger.

She had slept on a peapod with nine peas in it; she had squeezed an apple-pip between her fingers, and the pip had gone in the direction of her lover's house; but despite these favourable omens she is forced to repeat her sad complaint, "And ah this cruel Roger comes not yet." She had burnt nuts at Hallow-e'en, and Roger's nut burnt "right bonnily . . . nor flinch'd a-bit"; she had thrown turnip rinds into the air which had fallen, as they inevitably do, in a curve. (She was prepared to gloss this in a favourable way, however, because "she cawt it like a C—but cawt not true.") She had paid a fortune-teller who had comforted her with generalities, and at a wedding the unmarried girls had tested with a stocking who should marry next, but "ah this cruel Roger comes not yet."

Everything that could be done had been done, and at last common sense and hunger prevailed. There was no Keatsian banquet waiting outside for her, but the temptation was great.

> Thrice to her head she rais'd the luncheon brown
> Thrice lick'd her lips and three times laid it down;
> Purpos'd at length the very worst to prove:
> 'Twas easier sure to dye of ought than love.

Although Relph is very well aware of the foolishness of these antics, he does not mock at them. He maintains a friendly gravity that carries him very unaffectedly and happily through the poem. A similar wit and delicacy of execution is not to be found in the poem from which Relph probably derived the idea for his verses, *Thursday—The Spell*, from Gay's *The Shepherd's Week*.

Like Barnes's, Relph's poems are supplemented by a glossary of unfamiliar dialect words. From this list one gathers he had many of the same interests as Barnes more than a century later. Semasiology and antiquarianism were the hobbies of these poetical ministers, and a slightly anachronistic flavour can consequently be discovered in the poetry of them both. Examples are the use of such Old English survivals as *wood* for mad, and *ondergang* for undergo. His definition of *beck* ("a Rivulet or small Brook. A word common to the antient Saxon, high and low Dutch, and Danish") shows his interest in derivations. Most of the words in Relph's glossary are purely local jargon; many of them are vivid and immediately comprehensible ("*sweels of laughter*"); some have no particular advantage over their equivalent in normal usage (*dubbler*: platter; *gursin*: pasture). The list is not long, and the intrusion of unaccustomed words into the verse is not great, while the use of the dialect gives Relph so much more ease and charm of expression, that beyond doubt he was right in using it. Apart from the Scottish writers, who, under Allan Ramsay, then as always were pursuing an independent course, Relph was the first to use an English dialect as a poetic form since the days before the language had become unified.

Except as a forerunner Relph is of little importance compared with the greatest English dialect poet, William Barnes. It happened that Barnes was born in the first year of the nineteenth century, but the dates of his life and works are singularly irrelevant in considering his poetry. He was as isolated and independent of external influence as any poet that has ever written. The sea of faith might ebb or flow, passions might be stirred and intellects perplexed, but Barnes continued to live a tranquil and happy life in the Vale of Blackmore. Dorsetshire was his microcosm, and the intellectual isolation in which he lived unnoticed was to him a calm but complete unit of existence. Tennyson, who, after having drawn the elderly Barnes into uneasy speculations on Darwin and Pantheism, commented "he is not accustomed to strong views theologic," might have extended his statement without confining it to theology.

Barnes's retirement was not occasioned by misanthropy, but because he needed to be withdrawn in order to judge things in their simplicity and fitness. The beautiful and the good (terms that in his poetry would never be left naked in their abstraction) were to be found in nature, and through nature in art. Their virtues would be evident from the harmony and accord that were inherent in them. The craft of interpretation was a timeless one; and Barnes in his restrained artistry had much of the classicist in him, in the minute clarity of his observation something of Pre-Raphaelite brilliance, and in his ability to use the inanimate in nature as a touchstone for human feeling he held a key to Romanticism. But he would acknowledge no master except Homer, and no influences from poets in his own tongue. He was, as Patmore described him, "of no school but that of Nature."

The biography of Barnes lacks the pathos of a peasant-poet struggling for fame. Such attention as he did, belatedly, attract he did not solicit, and ambition was but one of the strong passions that had no part in his life. His father was a farmer in the Vale of Blackmore, in Dorset, and William in due course was sent to a nearby Dame's School where he received a rudimentary education, and displayed an enthusiasm for learning that made him parochially noticeable. Having left school Barnes's ability to write gained him a post in a solicitor's office, and gave him time to pursue his exceedingly eclectic bents. He studied Persian and Hindustani, explored the intricacies of Welsh poetry, and wrote a diary in Italian. His interests extended to mechanics and mathematics, in which he was something of an inventor, for he succeeded in making an instrument to describe ellipses, and with less success, an ingenious pair of swimming-shoes. He played the flute, violin, and piano, made chessmen on a lathe, and produced engravings after the manner of Bewick. These are but some of the astonishing variety of interests that Barnes displayed from an early age.

As might be expected the solicitor's office was soon exchanged for the village school. But schoolmastering in a rural district gave Barnes little opportunity to meet or converse with his peers. He himself was shy and awkward, but not, by any interpretation, naïve or ignorant. Yet in his love of the countryside and of domestic pursuits he was a voluntary exile from all contemporary intellectual contacts. Barnes married, became prematurely bald, was a humane disciplinarian (and consequently a popular schoolmaster), and settled down to live amongst a small circle of friends of intellectually low stature.

Barnes's literary activity was hardly less diverse than his other enthusiasms. During his days as a schoolmaster he wrote comedies for the local theatre (none of them is preserved), and published privately in Dorchester a small volume of verses, and *Orra, a Lapland Tale*. Neither of these productions is particularly memorable, although they contain the seeds of the brightness, clarity, and selectivity of colour that were to appear in his later works.

Barnes's chief occupation during his early pedagogical career was to write school-books. These ranged in subject between geography and etymology, perspective and Roman numerals, Aesop and Hindu fakirs. At first they were privately printed, but later he contributed his random thoughts to such periodicals as *The Gentleman's Magazine*. At one time Barnes even considered writing "a work of fiction," and was only deterred for lack of a plot.

Barnes possessed that rare combination, an ever-gleaning mind and a fluent pen. In his activities he was nearest, perhaps, to the complete man of the Renaissance, to whom no knowledge was worthless or unattainable in whatever field of learning it lay. Gradually, however, his interests crystallized, not towards poetry, which always remained to him "simply a refreshment of mind from cares and irksomeness," but towards philology. It was this enormous mistake in what he conceived to be his vocation that sheltered Barnes from the notice of the world for so long. When he was over sixty years of age Coventry Patmore discovered him, and announced that he "appears to consider that his *forte* lies in philology and antiquarianism, and to be endowed with a naïve ignorance of the fact that he is one of our very first poets." But before this his local reputation as a poet was well established. His verse readings were always well-attended, for his poetry was immediately comprehensible, written as it was in the dialect of his neighbourhood, and about scenes and incidents familiar to all who lived in that locality.

In 1847 Barnes was ordained deacon, and next year priest. After a short term of residence he received his degree of Bachelor of Divinity from Cambridge in his fiftieth year. But it was only a small, donative parish that he obtained, and not until twelve years later did the living at Winterbourne Came, which he had long desired, fall to him. Thereafter he never departed far or willingly from his birthplace, the Vale of Blackmore. Here he created his own Palace of Art, and as no one so inconvenient as Darwin or Bishop Colenso came to Dorset, he remained mentally unperplexed and created poetry (amongst other things) refreshing by reason of its lack of bewilderment. Barnes was never a part of the day-to-day world. Fifteen years after Thoreau had published *Walden* he replied to a letter from an American friend: "You have in one of your poems the name Walden, the name of a householder, a dairyman of this parish." Barnes's whole attitude of mind was that of a parochial antiquarianist. This attitude remained with him, for in his old age he once exclaimed indignantly, having just heard the word "bicycle," "why don't you call it 'wheel-saddle'?"

With the poetry of his contemporaries, or even of his predecessors, Barnes was supremely unconcerned. "I do not want," he said, "to be trammelled with the thoughts and styles of other poets, and I take none as my model except the Persian and Italian authors." It is true of him, more than of any other poet, that he hammered out his own method of poetic expression alone and without guidance. How out of touch he was with contemporary opinion may be gathered from his sincere praise of Waller's wit and good manners, and the greater interest he displayed in the Tonga paddle songs, called Towolo, or the three qualifications of poetry in the Welsh bardic canon, than in the fact that poets of no mean ability were writing in his own language. Therefore, as Mr. Grigson in his recent edition of Barnes's poems has pointed out, he borrowed from the literature of Ireland the under-rhyme (as in *Times o' Year*), from the Persians he imitated the matching of sounds in half lines—a sort of rhyming pun (as in *The Wold Wall*), from the Hebrew he took psalmic parallelism (as in *Melhill Feast*), and from the Welsh, in anticipation of Hopkins, he used a repetition of the same consonants in half-lines, split by a caesura. In short, as Mr. Grigson remarks, "he created a system of poetry for his own use."

It is difficult to know which of Barnes's diverse activities to approach first. To consider him as a poet without a knowledge of his background as a scholarly antiquarian would not do him justice. We must therefore glance at his more painstaking, though less permanent works in philology before passing to the recreation in which his true genius lay. Even in the study of antiquities and languages Barnes had the eagerness and (often misdirected) enthusiasm of the talented amateur. When a sewer was dug through his garden he triumphantly retrieved a bone hairpin and a stone stud; in a series of articles in *The Ladies' Treasury* on the art of adornment, he devoted one to the subject of tattooing. But in more serious vein Barnes produced a great quantity of philologically weighty material, which he published, at no great profit to himself (he never looked on publication as in any way an addition to his income), either in the learned periodicals or as independent books. It was the age of Max Müller, and certainly after the publication of *Tiw: or, a View on the roots and stems of the English as a Teutonic tongue*, Barnes could claim the doubtful reputation of being an English chip from Müller's German workshop.

The first and greatest of Barnes's learned works is his *Philological Grammar*, with the grandiose sub-title, "formed from a comparison of more than sixty languages." The first page contains a list of them. It includes such a diversity as Maeso-Gothic, Wendish, Damulican, Khoordish, Greenlandish, Lazistanish, Cheremissian, Lapponic, and Bisaya. The sub-title might well have been "Babel." The Grammar itself is a compendium of enormous erudition: it is in effect a world Grammar. As may be imagined it is highly complicated, yet Barnes had an orderly mind, and everything is carefully and methodically classified. In the sections on Prosody and Rhyme, probably the most pertinent to our immediate study, may be seen in the original those many poetic attributes that Barnes took from other languages to incorporate into his own poetry. But the critics fought shy of his weighty and laborious Grammar, which (in the phrase of his aggrieved daughter), "found but little favour with the general reader."

Barnes was undeterred, and his next book, *Tiw*, was if anything even more difficult to comprehend. More interesting, and closely connected with his use of dialect words was his *Grammar and Glossary of the Dorset Dialect*, later expanded as *A Glossary of the Dorset Dialect, with a Grammar of its Word Shapening and Wording*. "The Dorset has more freedom than has the more straitly bound book-speech," he claimed, and proceeded to justify his dialect as a "pure well of English undefiled." After a history of South-West English from earliest times, Barnes demonstrates the Dorset dialect by translating (with an impishness that we are to see in his poetry) the Queen's Speech from the Throne into a highly irreverent brogue. Her Majesty, for example, "do trust that theäse fruits mid be a-took, as proofs that the wealth-springs o' the land ben't aweakened."

The nature of the Grammar is again best seen by examining a small section in detail. Pronouns, for instance. "Whereas Dorset men are laughed at for what is taken as their misuse of pronouns," Barnes writes, "yet the pronouns of true Dorset, are fitted to one of the finest outplannings of speech that I have found." Here Barnes's dialectal pride, and disconcerting use of invented phrases to describe parts of speech (even more noticeable in his later works), is apparent. He continues to tell how "Full shapen things" (such as trees, tools, etc.), have a personal class of pronoun, *he*, with an accusative, *en*; whereas "unshapen quantities" of stuff have an impersonal class of pronoun, *it*. In the demonstratives, the personal class is *theäse* and *thick*; the impersonal, *this* and *that*. There are, therefore, Barnes proudly announces, four demonstratives in Dorset, but only two in English.

The "Glossary of the Dorset Dialect," which Barnes appends to his Grammar, contains some of the most memorable words and usages that any phrase-book can offer. Some are more beautiful than their original (Daffidowndilly: Daffodil), many are more pungent (Magoty: Fanciful. Slommock: A Slatternly Woman). Some of these usages are now almost common speech: (Baffle, Blether, Piggy-Back, Cubby-Hole); all of them are highly expressive. Certain phrases are peculiar to the local way of life (Sholduerens: Cider made from stolen apples carried home on the shoulders), and a majority concern the objects of common sight, often used to materialize abstractions (To owl about:

To wander by night), or to incorporate local lore [Pissabed: Dandelion ("said to be very diuretic, whence its name")]. Certainly the Glossary is a list to linger over, and Barnes's free use of such words is a great part of the fascination of his poetry. Barnes cannot be said to use a plain style when such decorative words are incorporated.

In *An Outline of English Speech-Craft* Barnes once more picks up the Anglo-Saxon cudgels (he had previously published a Grammar of that language), this time in favour of ousting foreign, in favour of native, words from the language. Some of his most memorable suggestions are, Soaksome (for Bibulous), Wort-lore (for Botany), and Folkdom (for Democracy). The book was a favourite of its author's, but its recommendations can scarcely be taken seriously. Barnes must have had sympathy with the boy in his own school who "scrope out the 'p' in psalm 'cos he didn't spell nothen."

The last of Barnes's serious works was written in his eightieth year (though those here mentioned are of necessity selective, since his output was enormous). *An Outline of Rede-Craft* is a study in Logic, which by the extreme anglicization of its style was written in a language of its own. Thus a syllogism becomes a "Three-Stepped Rede-ship," a proposition a "Thought-Putting," and a dilemma a "Two-Horned Redeship."

It is strange when one turns from Barnes the Philologist, contorted in semantic pedantries, to find Barnes the Poet without emotional or psychological subtleties, without an axe to grind, but occupied with simple, elemental feelings. He himself claimed in an unpublished fragment of autobiography, that "matters most interesting to me are those belonging to man, in his life of body, mind and soul, so in his speech, manners, laws and works." Barnes never strayed outside his native valleys to pursue this study, and it is with deep and benevolent satisfaction, not rapture, that he surveys the prospects around him. The men and women with whom he daily associated are the centre of his world, and he sees nature through them. The interdependence of man and nature, not on the spiritual level that Wordsworth describes it, but tangibly in every action of the countryman, has never been more acutely realized. Out of doors in the May sunshine that Barnes loved so dearly there is harmony between the earth and its inhabitants:

An' vields where chaps do vur outdo
The Zunday sky, wi' cwoats o' blue;
An' maïdens' frocks do vur surpass
The whitest deäsies in the grass.

The first poems Barnes wrote were in ordinary speech, and throughout his life he continued to produce such poetry side by side with his
dialect poems, and with no more pretensions to an elevated style or
theme. He claimed that he wrote in dialect because he could not help
it. "It is my mother tongue and is to my mind the only true speech
of the life that I draw." It is very probable, however, that the spirit of
the philologist caused him to write in Dorset. Unlike Doughty, who
consciously attempted to re-create sixteenth-century English, and
failed, Barnes, although starting as a perversity, ended by using it so
naturally that he even preached in the dialect.

There is an astonishing unity in a poem by Barnes. It is impossible
to capture the flavour of the whole from a few lines, and for this
reason almost all those who have written about him either do not
quote, or else reproduce an entire poem. No signal beauties arrest the
reader, although the effect of the entirety is undeniably fine. This is
caused largely by the rigidity of the form, coupled with the simplicity
of the effect. It kept Barnes to a high, even standard of verse-making.
He did not indulge in the visionary hit-and-miss brilliance of Clare,
although there is a similarity to Clare's

I found the poems in the fields,
And only wrote them down,

in Barnes's assertion, "I write pictures which I see in my mind."

Harmony was Barnes's watchword; and his poems are consequently
as indivisible as a fugue. He wrote for *The Gentleman's Magazine* on
harmonic proportions as applied to churches, he bound his books
harmonically, and he held that poetry must harmonize and conform
to nature. His study of harmony led to his belief that nature never
makes mistakes, and induced him to get together a collection of
the tints that nature most frequently contrasts, which he attempted to
introduce into both his painting (another of his pastimes) and his
poetry. Consequently there is a frequent use of colour-words in

Barnes's verse, often contrasted in pairs, but always simple; blue, yellow or white.

> The gookoo over white-weav'd seas
> Do come to zing in thy green trees;

or again in his description of *The Water Crowvoot*,

> Thy beds o' snow-white buds do gleam
> So feäir upon the sky-blue stream.

His colour descriptions are not so lavish as those of his contemporaries the Pre-Raphaelites, but there is an aloof calmness in his descriptions that elevates his poetry, despite its fetters of loam, above the normal run of nature poets.

In his article, *Thoughts on Beauty and Art*, Barnes repeats the well-known formula, used indiscriminately by Pope, Cowper, and Wordsworth, "Nature is the best school of art," but adds as a corollary of his own, "and of schools of art among men those are best that are nature's best interpreters." His poetry is an able defence of his theory, and many vivid images, brilliant yet simple, spring to mind; the "loose-limbed rest of infants," "thin-heäir'd cows" that

> up bezide the mossy raïls
> Do stan' an' zwing their heavy taïls,

"the high-wound zongs o' nightingeäles," or the

> whitest clouds, a-hangèn high
> Avore the blueness o' the sky.

In Patmore's words, "the Life of Nature has seldom flowed with more surprising and enchanting freedom."

Not one of Barnes's poems is of any great length and none contains hidden meanings; they are all plain and downright. They depict the countryman in all the aspects of his life, at all seasons, working, courting, mourning, as he is still to be found in the flesh. Barnes's realism is never tempered by harshness, as is that of the poet of the East Anglian scene, Crabbe. He has no unkind words for anyone, largely because he does not sit in judgment. There is an utter lack of personal intrusion on the poet's part. He is always the sympathetic observer, watching the human kaleidoscope against a background of pastoral simplicity. Loss of intense power is inevitable, and whereas Barnes may be pathetic and charming in his descriptions, he never greatly moves one, and can but produce an evanescent delight. As he told the Bishop of Salisbury who visited him in his old age, all he had written was true of someone in the classes described in his poems, and he had painted from life even though the level might have been above the average.

The Welsh triad that Iolo Morganwg had long before advised the poets and critics of his generation to study was rediscovered by Barnes, who attempted to follow the discipline that is demanded of a man of *awen*, or poetic genius. Such a man, Iolo declared, must possess "an eye that can see Nature; a heart that can feel Nature; and a resolution that dares follow Nature." The triad did not require a poet to interpret nature; consequently Barnes is not often didactic, and then only unobtrusively. He will indicate his message (often using one of his characters to do this, not himself), but never press it.

> An' vok' do come, an' live, an' goo,
> But rivers don't gi'e out, John.

For the most part he sang for the pure joy of song. It was this aspect of his work that made Patmore draw a comparison between him and Theocritus—a comparison that had been lavished on Bloomfield forty years before. But Barnes does not describe a golden, pastoral age; his Muse is lowlier than the Sicilian's; it never soars so high. He was always unambitiously in command. Of Barnes's poems Hopkins said, "it is true they are not far-fetched or exquisite . . . but they are straight from nature and quite fresh."

There is no question that Barnes's dialect poems are those on which his fame most justifiably rests. We have already seen some of the perils that a dialect poet must face, avoiding preciosity on the one hand and incomprehensibility on the other. Relph being unknown, only the Scots had succeeded in making poetry out of local speech. Barnes was the first to prove that his Dorset dialect was more than an antiquarian curiosity. Hopkins, despite the lavish praise that he bestowed on Barnes's poetry, was not fully convinced that the dialect added to, or was even an integral part of, its poetic merit. "You may translate them and they are nearly as good," he claimed, and he agreed with Bridges that the dialect gave "a peculiar but short-lived charm." This might be true if Barnes had the slightest pretensions towards a poetic diction, but, unlike Wordsworth, his language was indeed the language of common speech. His lines cry out to be read with a West Country burr, regardless of whether the inflections are printed or imagined by the reader. The dialect is in large measure the very texture of the verse, and the colloquial passages in particular would be lost without it. The following lines, for example, it would be impossible to render into common speech without making them as bathetic as *Simon Lee* or *Alice Fell*.

> The tiaties must be ready purty nigh;
> Do tiake oone up upon a fark an' try,
> The kiake upon the vier too's aburnen,
> I be afeärd: do run an' zee, an' turn en.

Although in the mechanics of poetry Barnes was a highly-trained artist, he had at the same time no artistic pedigree. As Patmore observed Barnes might well have written as he did had no other poet ever lived. But as he shunned fame, and had no gospel to preach (other than to his congregation at Winterbourne Came), he attracted no public notice until he was over sixty years of age, when he was rewarded by the admiring attentions of a small cabal of poets—Hardy, Patmore, and Hopkins—and a small pension of £70 a year. With this Barnes was perfectly content, nor did ambition stir within him. Duck and Bloomfield were lionized and perhaps spoilt as poets; Barnes continued to administer to his parish, scythe his lawn in a pale-blue dressing-gown, and pursue his studies in semantics.

So even was the tenor of his life that apart from his very earliest works it is impossible to trace any development in his poetry. Those poems that he wrote as a youth, felicitous in their descriptions of childhood and young love, are indistinguishable from those he continued to write into old age. He seems to have been born with this limited but perfect gift of expression, which persisted with as unwavering a flame as his own essential humanity. "There is no art without love," he wrote in that memorable essay on Beauty and Art, which contains his whole creed of aesthetics, "every artist who has produced anything worthy has had a love of his subject." Barnes's love was very deep, yet he never sentimentalizes, because of his detachment, and because of the gruff, earthy quality that dialectal good sense always creates. They are manly poems, albeit often exceedingly delicate, and they are poems that need to be sung; they are always (except certain of the humorous verses) of an entrancing lyricism. Hopkins sensed this when he set two of them to music. Barnes wrote to be read aloud: the printed word scarcely does him justice. The seeming cacophony of certain phrases does not occur in spoken Dorset, where speech is soft and burred, like humble-bees ("Dumbledores" in the Glossary) in a clover-field.

In speaking about Barnes I have not allowed Barnes to speak for himself. It is a significant fact, and one that Patmore also realized in his essay on the poet. The lack of illustrative quotations in these pages is primarily due to the unity of the poems; they do not present the critic with fragments that will fairly represent the whole. Barnes fashioned his work with such care and restraint, that in justice to him, and also to indicate a few of the innumerable ingenious rhythms and metres he employed, a few of his poems should be printed in their entirety. They are not necessarily the best, but they are representative of his outpourings.

My Orcha'd in Linden Lea, familiar to many in its musical setting, is one of the loveliest of Barnes's descriptive poems, and expresses in its final verse the essence of his love of retirement.

> 'Ithin the woodlands, flow'ry gleäded,
>   By the woak tree's mossy moot,
> The sheenèn grass-bleädes, timber-sheäded,
>   Now do quiver under voot;
> An' birds do whissle auver head,
> An' water's bubblèn in its bed,
> An' there vor me the apple tree
> Do leän down low in Linden Lea.
>
> When leaves that leätely were a-springèn
>   Now do feäde 'ithin the copse,
> An' painted birds do hush their zingèn
>   Up upon the timber's tops;

An' brown-leav'd fruit's a-turnèn red,
In cloudless zunsheen, auver head,
Wi' fruit vor me, the apple tree
Do leän down low in Linden Lea.

Let other vo'k meäke money vaster
    In the aïr o' dark-room'd towns,
I don't dread a peevish meäster;
    Though noo man do heed my frowns,
I be free to goo abrode,
Or teäke ageän my hwomeward road
To where, vor me, the apple tree
Do leän down low in Linden Lea.

Jeän is one of the many autobiographical poems that Barnes wrote about his own wife. He wrote of young love, of married love, and the unhappy memories of a love who has departed, for Julia Barnes died thirty-four years before him. That her memory never left him may be judged from the constant record of his grief in his Italian diary. "Giulia" he wrote at the end of each day's entry after her death.

We now mid hope var better cheer,
My smilèn wife o' twice vive year.
Let others frown, if thee bist near
    Wi' hope upon thy brow, Jeän;
Var I vust lov'd thee when thy light
Young shiape vust grow'd to woman's height;
I lov'd thee near, an out o' zight,
    An' I da love thee now Jeän.

An we've a-trod the sheenen bliade
Ov eegrass in the zummer shiade,
An' when the leaves begun to fiade
    Wi' zummer in the wiane, Jeän;
An' we've a-wander'd droo the groun'
O' swayen wheat a-turnen brown,
An' we've a-stroll'd together roun'
    The brook, an' droo the liane, Jeän.

An' nuone but I can ever tell
Ov al thy tears that have a-vell
When trials miade thy buzzom zwell,
　An' nuone but thee o' mine, Jeän;
An' now my heart, that heav'd wi' pride
Back then to have thee at my zide,
Da love thee muore as years da slide,
　An' leäve thae times behine, Jeän.

There seems no obvious reason why *Melhill Feast* is written in
Queen's English rather than in Dorset, but the verses from it that
follow serve as an interesting comparison, and show how inter-
changeably Barnes's talents could be applied within the limited range
of his subject-matter. The line, "By glittering gossamer and dew,"
might be objected to as too consciously poetic. Nevertheless, in this
instance and elsewhere the words employed are of Saxon origin, and
foreign importations, which Barnes hated, are rigorously excluded
from his writings. This limits his vocabulary, but it is also a form of
insurance. The words he does employ are more absolute in their
meaning, more appropriate when applied to the protagonists of the
poems, and have a wholesomeness and honesty about them that a
mixed vocabulary might mar. Barnes's purpose in simplifying was
also to unify the English tongue, and his is perhaps the ideal compromise between the languages of high and low life in limiting the
vocabulary when writing about "low" subjects to words that are in
common use by the characters, the author and the reader.

Aye, up at the feast, by Melhill's brow,
So softly below the clouds in flight,
There swept on the wood, the shade and light,
Tree after tree, and bough by bough.

And there, among girls on left and right,
On one with a winsome smile, I set
My looks; and the more, the more we met
Glance upon glance, and sight by sight.

The road she had come by then was soon
The one of my paths that best I knew,
By glittering gossamer and dew,
Evening by evening, moon by moon.

Sweet were the hopes I found to cheer
My heart as I thought on time to come,
With one that would bless my happy home,
Moon upon moon, and year by year.

A final example of Barnes's craft as a poet is one of his humorous verses. He was a skilful raconteur, and in this instance his brilliant use of idiom and childlike artlessness make a very happy parable from the recollected incident.

When I wer' still a bwoy, an' mother's pride,
A bigger bwoy spoke up to me so kind-like,
"If you do like, I'll treat ye wi' a ride
In theäse wheel-barrow here." Zoo I wer' blind-like
To what 'e had a-workèn in his mind-like,
An' mounted vor a passenger inside;
An' comèn to a puddle, perty wide,
He tipp'd me in, a-grinnèn back behind-like.
Zoo when a man do come to me so thick-like,
An' sheäke my hand, where oonce 'e pass'd me by,
An' tell me he would do me this or that,
I can't help thinkèn o' the big bwoy's trick-like.
An' then, vor all I can but wag my hat
An' thank en, I do veel a little shy.

Barnes's poetry is the embodiment of a way of life, and in a tradition that we cannot hope to share. Inevitably we read him at a remove, for to analyse it minutely is only to destroy "the many-coloured thing." Barnes nevertheless deserves to be read, though we must expect to lose much of the bloom in gathering the fruit. It is not the difficulty of the language, which hardly interferes with fluent reading at all, but something more subtle; an attitude of mind. Barnes's poetry demands of the reader a compatibility of simplicity and dignity, enthusiasm without patronage, and a sincere parochial love of humanity. Neither the reader nor the poet is expected to do more than watch the scene sympathetically. The poetry does not induce tears or emotion, but it warms one with unaffected delight.

Alfred Williams

Though I am in great company
Yet walk I in deep solitude,
For plenty is in poverty,
And famine in the multitude.

ALFRED WILLIAMS: *My Soul is Free as Ambient Air*

There is a story told of the childhood of Alfred Williams that is a strange, but not inappropriate, introduction to the life of a country poet enmeshed in an industrial age. The railway-line from London to Swindon and the West Country passed within a mile of the village of South Marston where Williams was born, and although the boy delighted in the flowers and birds of the Wiltshire downlands he was sufficiently a child of his times to be equally attracted by the trains. Once he lay down between the rails and waited until a goods train had passed over him.

The incident may be read as a symbol of Williams's working life. He remained a free spirit, but voluntarily subjugated himself to an industry unnatural to him by birth and temperament. He was called the Hammerman Poet, but it is seldom indeed that the Swindon railway workshop features in his poetry. Like so many of his labouring-class village companions better pay (pitifully inadequate as it now seems) drew him to the town; but his heart was never captured by the forge or the allurements of cinema and skating-rink. The fields and villages in the Vale of the White Horse and the slow, honest life that was lived there were to him poetry and the very breath of his own existence.

Clare could not endure a physical separation from Helpstone, but Bloomfield might have understood more readily how Williams could take with him those things that were most precious, and find solace by remembering them in exile. But neither Clare nor Bloomfield lived in an age when industrialization actively encroached upon country life. Certainly they would have fled from it. For Williams the age of machines represented a challenge to his sensibilities as a poet, and on the last day of his employment he chalked *vici* on the plate over the furnace where he worked. It was a victory; but it was the victory of a single, indomitable man who entered the factory a countryman, and left as a poet of the countryside. The victory for poetry itself is still being sought, when the machines themselves will offer up a Muse.

Alfred Williams was born in 1877, the fifth of eight children. He never knew his father, who abandoned his wife and family when Alfred was still a child. His mother undertook the heavy responsibilities of raising her family with no more money than she could earn by delivering papers, selling sweets and taking in needlework. As soon as the children were of an age to be helpful they were employed in the daily struggle for bread, and it is scarcely surprising that their formal education was brief and perfunctory. At the age of eight Alfred was at school for only half the day, and spent the remainder of his time, like Giles before him, doing odd jobs for a local farmer. In this way he earned two shillings a week, and learned to love not so much the specific occupations of farming but the environment in which they were carried out.

At the age of eleven he left school for good, and worked under a number of farmers in the district for five years. He was restless and impetuous by nature, and quite untouched by the quest for learning that dominated his adult life. He saved up to buy a telescope, tried to enlist in the Navy, and finally, like his brothers and so many of his village friends, undertook the four-mile walk into Swindon and the railway factory.

It was a strange, and in many ways an unhappy, choice. Factory work was better paid and, although he never availed himself of it, offered better opportunity for advancement than agriculture. In the early days, before literature and learning occupied his thoughts, he may have been more ambitious and hoped to progress through the stamping shop to more congenial employment; but once he had become aware of his own creative powers he never attempted to improve his conditions of work. Until ill-health forced him to retire he worked conscientiously, but without enthusiasm, as a steam-hammerman. He endured rather than accepted an arduous and unprofitable job, but stubbornly refused to search for an alternative. Partly through pride, and partly through preoccupation, he kept separate the physically-exhausting, nine-hour working day, and husbanded his mind for the self-imposed mental tasks that he wrestled with by night and in the early mornings.

A machine-ridden life, Williams found, exercised a subtle domination over the free spirit of man. It was a challenge that never frightened him, but it needed to be constantly and actively fought. In his own life he played the part of Penelope, unthreading by night the stitches that he had worked at all day. It was double labour, but through it he preserved his own proud moral integrity. After nearly twenty years at the railway factory he was able to view with complete clarity the relative advantages of an industrial and an agricultural worker's life. He knew both by experience, and in his preface to *A Wiltshire Village* he leaves no doubt as to his own predilection. Williams's intellect could despise the life's labour of his body, but he was neither angered nor frustrated by the analysis. He was sincere both in denouncing the form of work in which he was engaged, and in striving, even against doctor's advice, to continue performing it. The method he adopted of earning a living was of small consequence compared to his sustained recognition of the true values of life itself.

I cannot conceal my love of the country-side, and a boundless admiration for, and sympathy with, the humble folk who till the soil, harvest the crops, and tend the cattle; who are free from the shackles of town life, and content to dwell in peace away from the din and turmoil, the strife and battle, of the streets and factories. It has been my lot to labour in the fields and in the factory, too, to be both rural and urban, to have knowledge of two spheres, and two sets of conditions. I have driven the plough, milked the cows, made hay, and harvested the corn with the farmer and his men, and I have toiled and groaned long years at the furnace and steam-hammer, in the midst of ten thousand workmen; but though in it, I was never of it, and, try as I will, I cannot find many good words to say for the manufacturing life. Higher wages there may be, and slightly shorter hours, and a few other "privileges"—a bigger house to live in, perhaps, with more games and amusements, but they can never compensate one for the unnatural confinement in the smoke, and stench, and gloom, week after week, and year after year; for the fever and fret, and heart-gripings, wasting health, and sense of despair and utter helplessness that grows upon the individual there; and, above all, the loss to character, of sound healthy principles, hardihood, the power to battle with life and circumstance, and that jewel, so easily lost and hardly recovered—simplicity of taste, thought, method, and objective. After five years of town or factory life the ordinary man is incapable of rustic conditions and occupations; he feels to be bound body and soul to the industrial area, he cannot leave it any more.

When Williams was twenty he took up reading as a serious occupation. Usually his enthusiasms were intense but short-lived; painting and politics had taken their turn at filling his hours of leisure. Literature supplanted these, and all other, pursuits to become his single domination and his love. At first he would carry a play by Shakespeare around in his pocket, but within a year or two his interest had grown so much that he enrolled in a four-year correspondence course from Ruskin College, Oxford.

The Industrial Revolution, that was anathema to the peasant-poet, brought with it systems of adult education that would have unquestionably benefited the ill-educated but aspiring countryman. Ruskin College, which had just been founded in 1899, provided Williams with opportunities for self-advancement that Duck or Bloomfield, living in a less mechanized age, would have dearly loved. The centuries passed without perceptibly easing the lot of the countryman, and although the industrial age introduced new encroachments it brought some compensations, too.

The correspondence course taught Williams much and whetted his appetite for more. "Life would not be worth living without my literature; I love it," he declared. His waking life was subjected to such a stringent self-discipline that none but the most ardent of lovers could have stood the physical strain. It was not his nature to master one thing at a time. The Ruskin College survey of English literature had made him aware of his ignorance of Latin, and he set about repairing the deficiency straightway. Next London Matriculation seemed desirable, and this required, in addition to English and Latin, a knowledge of Greek, French and Mathematics. Each new subject Williams undertook with so much exhilaration and diligence that one almost forgets the long working day at the forge, and the daily bicycle journey between Swindon and South Marston. There was time, too, at the week-end for excursions into the surrounding countryside, and even time to get married and set up house in the village of his birth.

Mary Peck had been a childhood friend of Alfred Williams, and although herself unintellectual and of a retiring nature her unwavering loyalty and quiet endurance of privation made possible her husband's constant dedication. Her rewards were small. She never saw her partner achieve the success that their few constant friends assured her was his due, she was not blessed with children, and she saw little enough of Alfred himself, whose books were more demanding of his time than she was. "While she knits," wrote Williams, "I commune with my gods." In the early days of their married life he would rise at four in the morning and study for an hour or two before setting out for work, with a book in his pocket to occupy his lunch-hour. Every evening he would cycle home for supper, and continue working far into the night. "I took care to cram in as much as possible under all circumstances," he observed.

A desperate earnestness in the quest for knowledge is a commendable, but not always an endearing, quality. Life was unkind to Williams: frequently it was cruel. He faced the buffets of fortune with a humourless, inflexible determination. His Welsh-bred tenacity allowed no compromise or deviation from the course he had ordained for himself. He spared neither himself nor his wife in his passage through life. But the fanaticism that renders his biography merely pitiful is mellowed in his poetry by that unassuming humility with which nature endows her true lovers. The countryside displayed the richness of his spirit; the town only accentuated the poverty of his circumstances.

Soon after his marriage in 1903 Williams found that reading needed to be supplemented by writing. His interests at this time were largely in the classics, and his unpublished poetic play *Sardanapalus* was composed under their influence. Shorter poems, some original, some translations from the Latin or Greek, followed easily. Lyrical expression was not strange to him, for in the villages round South Marston folk-songs were still composed and sung, especially amongst the older generation, and the rhythms and expressions of song formed a natural background to his own compositions.

He achieved no immediate recognition. Publishers, then as now, were not anxious to print the verses of an unknown poet without a financial guarantee that Williams could not contemplate. At the factory his latest freak received some gibes, but for the most part Williams's dour silence dried up opposition and interest, and he was left alone by his fellow-workmen. For four or five years he continued to read and write without gaining any more substantial success than an occasional poem or article published in the local paper, or at best in an Authors' Association anthology.

Even these meagre outlets found him a few friends, especially amongst the closely-knit and loyal fraternity of uneducated poets with whom Williams's name must always be associated. There was Frederick Rockell, the first man publicly to recognize Williams's genius; William Dowsing of Sheffield, caught like Williams in the web of industrial life, and who rejoiced when the sales of his sonnets reached two figures; Jonathan Denwood, a Cumberland poet, who, like his father and brother, kept alive the traditions of dialect and peasant verse that Relph and blind John Stagg the fiddler had already established in the Lake District. Lastly, and nearest, perhaps, to Williams's heart, was Edward Slow, who composed and had printed in Salisbury an unceasing flow of garrulous stories in verse, written in the Wiltshire dialect that Williams knew and loved so well.

By 1909 the indifference that Williams had encountered for so long gave place to a modest public interest. *The Daily Telegraph* singled out two poems by Williams from an anthology of new verse, and declared that the author was "one of the most remarkable men in Wiltshire, if not in England." Better still, Williams first found a publisher and then a patron. Galloway Kyle, one of the founders of the publishing house "Erskine Macdonald" suggested that a collection of Alfred Williams's poems might be a suitable first publication for the new firm, and Lord Fitzmaurice, a philanthropic and friendly Wiltshire landowner, guaranteed the book against loss.

Songs in Wiltshire was received with the mild encouragement that reviewers usually accord to young poets, but which has little influence on the sales of the book. Erskine Macdonald failed to dispose of any substantial number, and Williams seemed faced by the prospect of calling in his guarantee. Already he had resolved to do no such thing, and undertook the job of selling his poems himself. Every day after work he would go off on his bicycle with copies of the book and hawk them from door to door in all the villages nearby as well as in Swindon itself. It was a strenuous, but in the end successful, expedient. Neither Lord Fitzmaurice nor Williams lost money on the book, and eventually the small edition was exhausted. But it had been hard work and Williams, not unnaturally, was disappointed by the lack of enthusiasm he had encountered, especially in his own neighbourhood. "It is a regrettable truth," he afterwards remarked to Lord Fitzmaurice, "but it has to be admitted, that poetry is going out of the lives of most people."

The poems in Williams's first volume are pleasing but not compulsive. Likenesses to the poetry of A. E. Housman spring immediately to mind; but these resemblances are superficial, for Williams has neither Housman's irony nor his economy of line and language. Williams's rhythms have something of Housman's buoyancy, and he expresses himself with the hearty outdoor vigour that is a sure herald of the Georgian literary mood.

> A thousand years will come and go,
>   And thousands more will rise,
> My buried bones to dust will grow,
>   And dust defile my eyes;
> But when the lark sings o'er the wold
>   And the swallow weaves her nest,
> My soul will take the coltsfoot gold
>   And blossom on thy breast.
>
> O thou bonny high hill!
>   I covet no other;
> Our secrets we tell
>   For we love one another.

Liddington Hill, from which this stanza is taken, is a more localized poem than the majority in the book. Wiltshire, though figuring on the title-page, is scarcely identifiable from the descriptions of that county in the verses that follow. It is strange, in view of the prose that Williams later wrote, that his gift of reportage was not more scrupulously employed. But it was not a regrettable chance. In his poetry he avoided the minute parochialism that constricts all judgment on his prose, and if his verses pall after sustained reading it is more from a monotony of bright chirruping than any intrinsic flaw. The outpouring of his songs, with their cascades of hyphenated descriptive words, and the breathless enthusiasm of discovered power over language, can be appreciated in a poem such as *The Blackbird's Canticle*.

> "Cher-a-peeke,
> Peeke, peeke, peeke," sung the blackbird,
> "All honour to the daisy, the daisy;
> The pale-green, yellow-hearted primrose;
> The blowing plumes of the crimson herb-sorrel;
> The green-robed fern, and mother hedge-parsley;
> Ruddy oak leaves, and crowns of poplar;
> Black ash, and silver leaves of the bramble;
> And the smooth-leaved smooth-rinded beeches;
> All the green-souled, green-tinted,
> Gold-leaved, and purple-mantled
> Impearled and imbrasured jewelry
> Of the bordered meadow and running streamlet,
> High wood and bellowing oak forest."

There is a thinner, more derivative strain apparent in some of his nature poetry that owes a debt to the Arcadian verses of the Elizabethans. But time gives no quaint gloss to Williams's conceits, and his lightest confections only emphasize his limitations of mood and sentiment. His love poems in particular lack grace and invention. At their best they rely more on landscape than human passion.

> 'Tis pleasant with my nut-brown lass,
>   When the autumn breezes blow,
> To tread the dewy meadow grass,
>   Cheerily, merrily O!
> To stoop amid the golden rust,
>   My sickle in my hand,
> And scatter the scarlet poppy-dust
>   That reddens all the land.

In his more serious poems Williams was often unfortunate in his choice of metres and rhythms. Throughout this early book he remained faithful to the lyrical song rhythms that he knew and loved best, despite their occasional incongruity. In his verses he seldom indulges in introspection or autobiography, but when he does speak from the heart it is with a compelling fervour. The finest poem in the book, *On the Downs*, strikes an elegiac note of mingled sorrow and beauty, with a dignity that only Hardy could excel.

> O my heart! the day has been
>   Full of bitter. Here we rest,
> Unobtruding and unseen;
>   Stretched upon the shaded green,
> Unpossessing, unpossest
>   With the burning scorn of anger,
> Yielding to divinest languor,
>   Dream we on the magic West.

Not all of the collection is as felicitous, for Williams was always a poet of uneven merit. There is a heavy weight of poems of fancy, often introducing, with a ponderousness that Housman could have taught him to avoid, Williams's newly gleaned knowledge of classical myth.

But Williams did not care to read much of the poetry of his contemporaries; he preferred Dryden and the classics. At the time of *Songs in Wiltshire*'s publication he looked through the poems of Bridges, Yeats, Hardy and some others, but declared that "this has produced in me a veritable disgust of modern '*tack*.'" If Williams did indeed develop his poetic gifts uninfluenced by his contemporaries, how powerful and unifying was the spirit of the age that could mould his utterances into such harmony with theirs. The years before the 1914–18 war were Indian summer for the robust poets of pastoral song. After the world conflict the temper of poetry changed, and Williams found his talent unadaptable. His life as a creative poet was short and had a dying fall: one wonders if he could have learnt resilience had he been less scornful of the idiom of his contemporaries, and more sensitive to change.

Williams's efforts with his first volume were scarcely over before he had a second book of poems ready for the printer. Once again he found that no publisher would accept it without a financial backing. Offers of support came from three directions, but Williams hated to be under any obligation, and although his wages at the railway factory only amounted to thirty shillings a week, he gambled on his success as a salesman and underwrote the production himself.

Poems in Wiltshire was published in 1911. Williams's talents were maturing quickly, and two years had added a breadth of experience and an ease of expression to his verses. His reading, too, had been widespread, as at times is apparent from poems written under the immediate influence of some particular author. One book, however, influenced him more than superficially and came to dominate his life and thought. In view of Williams's declaration, "all my being is concentered in this little plot of ground," it is not surprising that the author, Richard Jefferies, was a Wiltshireman, and the book, *The Story of my Heart*, had as its setting those same fields and downs that Williams also knew and loved. Both writers are now commemorated by the same monument, and, fittingly, it is erected on Barbury Hill where they had often passed the hours in solitude and meditation. Jefferies, "the earth-lover" as Williams called him, would surely have been glad to share this hilltop and Liddington nearby with the author of *Homeland*, whose natural responses were so closely akin to his own.

> Ofttimes on Liddington's bare peak I love to think and lie,
> And muse upon the former days and ancient things gone by.

The subjects and metres of Williams's latest poems were as diverse as ever, but it becomes increasingly obvious that he was least adept at set-pieces on, for example, *The Druidical Remains at Avebury*, and rhetorical, abstract ponderings on *Natural Thoughts and Surmises*. The flush of new learning that Williams was acquiring often had an unsettling influence on his poetry. It was tempting to use indiscriminately, and to give back to the world unaltered and undistilled, the wisdom that he had so recently gained. His best poetry was undoubtedly written after the subject had passed through the alembic of meditation during

> these solitary hours
> Dear-spent in Nature's silent company
> By dale, or down, or wooded sanctuary,
> Beneath blue heavens and firmaments.

With increased knowledge came an increased vocabulary, and Williams, either through excitement or inexperience, was prodigal in his use of words. Economy of expression is probably the last thing that a writer learns, and Williams may easily be forgiven his excesses. At times he seems almost to be stammering in his enthusiasm to express his precise meaning. When hyphens are put aside, and the very simplest thoughts are dressed in the simplest language, Williams can command a natural pathos that it is not inappropriate to compare with Wordsworth's early verse. *In my Garden* is one of the most controlled of these poems: in it he tells how a wren came to him as he was resting and eventually perched on his head. In a different style, but written also within the compass of his experience, is *In Sevenhampton Fields*, from a line or two of which Williams's knowledgeable affection for the natural world around him may be appreciated.

> Down by Sevenhampton's waving fields there flows
>   A gentle-minded stream with steady motion,
> That underneath the emerald-tinted boughs
>   Strives toward the drifting ocean.
>
> Blue with forget-me-not its banks appear,
>   And fragrant meadow-sweet and hawthorn bushes,
> The lovely golden iris blossoms here
>   And many-flowering rushes.

Williams's creative energies were now at their peak, and he supplemented his poetry-writing with two books of prose. The first, which was published some years later with the title *Life in a Railway Factory*, touched on matters concerning labour relations and politics that made it imprudent to publish while he was still employed at Swindon. Although he claimed to hold moderate opinions on such matters and did not "subscribe to the extreme views held by the Socialist-Labour people," Williams was highly critical of the conditions prevailing in the factory and the attitude of his employers. The radical and practical reforms he suggested were better received in 1915, when the book appeared, than he would have expected four years before, when it was first written.

The second prose work that he wrote was intended as a companion piece, and described in a digressive and anecdotal fashion the conditions and way of life in an agricultural village. The village he chose was, of course, South Marston, and Williams was confident that the truths he intended to reveal would prove as controversial as in the previous book. This was not the case. Duckworth unhesitatingly accepted the book for publication, and, with the exception of the vicar, the inhabitants of South Marston were more offended at having been left out of, than they were of being included in, the survey.

The Preface to *A Wiltshire Village* is an intelligently reasoned and remarkably dispassionate assessment of the relative advantages in the choice between town and country that faced the labouring class in Williams's day. His own sympathies lay with the countryman. "Highly intellectual he may not be," Williams conceded, "but he often discovers more soul and feeling than his town confrère; and he is usually more of a human being than the other, and a better *man*, in the true sense of the term." One cannot but wonder how such a judgment was received by Williams's workmates at the railway factory. He himself had very little to say about his personal relationships at work; but it can be gathered that he was aloof, taciturn, and not particularly popular. In the poem *The Testament* that he wrote at about this time he declared, with a touch of superiority that would have aggravated his fellow-workers all the more, "How they scorn the breath of my mouth, and very nearly laid hands upon me."

No more than this single line is necessary to show that Williams had been reading Whitman. It was an unfortunate influence, but a strong one. The comparative freedom from the discipline of stanzaic forms led him to attempt longer poems notable for their incongruous infusion of tin-trumpet pride. Most of Williams's poetry was modest and had an unpretentious charm, but *The Hill* and *The Testament*, with which he introduced his third book of verses, *Nature and Other Poems*, have a rhetorical arrogance about them that the shorter pieces that follow do not attempt to imitate.

> I am tired of streets and faces,
> When I walk between the high walls with the crowd pushing at my elbow,
> The old and young and middle-aged, laughing and talking together,
> That seem to be in love with their prison, almost enraptured with it.

The direct imitators of Whitman have little to recommend them poetically, and the chief interest in these longer poems of Williams's is with the philosophy of life that he tries to establish. Despite the boastfulness already mentioned (partly Whitman's and partly his own) his attitude remains surprisingly unacrimonious. The neglect of society for its poets and its workpeople was not reflected in his poetry. Jefferies had taught him to pay more regard to man's place in nature than in society, and his constant love for all the aspects of the external, natural world assumed an almost pantheistic fervour. "I follow Nature in all things; I was born natural," he asserted. The natural philosophy towards which he strove is implicit also in a number of the shorter lyrics, *After the Rain* being one of the most perfect.

Undertakings in both prose and verse continued to occupy Williams's time, and in 1913, as in the preceding year, he succeeded in getting published another book of poems, *Cor Cordium*, as well as *Villages of the White Horse*, a successor to his study of life and labour in South Marston, and covering this time "the life of a dozen villages from Wroughton to the Blowing Stone all along the downside"; the subject-matter was "dialect, folklore, and all sorts of quaint stuff, but especially attempting to depict the life and characteristics of the agricultural classes in that region."

Cor Cordium was the last of Williams's books of poetry to be published before the war, and it marks the climax of his poetic achievement. Indeed, apart from a brief reawakening of poetic inspiration some years later in circumstances that he never could have predicted, it contains the last noteworthy poetry that he wrote. It was not an entirely original volume, as it contained a number of lyrics that had already appeared in earlier books; but these he combined with new material to form a cycle of love songs, prefaced by a long, analytical poem, *Historia Cordis*.

Williams was of too solitary a disposition to write love songs from his own experience. His affection for his wife, Mary, was not of an inflammatory nature that breeds poetry in the heart. Neither had he the imagination to characterize or make physically credible an emotional partnership of which he was not an active participant. Barnes had the same detachment in his love poetry, but avoided the flatness from which Williams's lyrics sometimes suffer by more pointed dramatic situations or the gentlest use of irony. *Cor Cordium* is not, however, a featureless exercise in unfelt emotion. Williams wrote with a deep love, not of any individual but of the image of nature in human actions. *Love Unfaithful*, which is a fair representative of many others in this book, is a poem both of love and landscape.

> Her summer smile was sweeter
>   Than summer skies at morn;
> Her lightning glances fleeter
>   Than ever lightning born;
> The blue-bright fields above her
>   Were mirrored in her eyes,
> How could I help but love her,
>   So little wisdom-wise!
>
> The years waxed ever younger,
>   Stars thickened in the blue,
> And stronger yet and stronger
>   My doting passion grew;
> The green round world about her
>   New blossomed at her tread,
> The green round world without her
>   A thousand times were dead.
>
> Ah! simple, soulful-minded,
>   What utter woe was mine,
> Too darkly passion-blinded,
>   Too rich with lover's wine;
> There came a burst of anger,
>   Clouds crimson-lit with flame,
> My dreaming, still, soul-languor
>   Fast yielded up to shame.

Human relationships, Williams found, were often as precipitate and complicated as those he described in his poem; but storms in nature passed as they came without acrimony, spoiling nothing and changing nothing. It was to the happy constancy of such a world that Williams turned for consolation. After the daily wounds of life it was nature who doctored him,

> The healer of the heart, the doom of grief,
> Strong with the medicine of flower and leaf.

By 1914 Williams's ceaseless work began seriously to affect his health. He complained of violent pains about his heart, and was told that he should give up his job at the factory. He paid little attention to his doctor's advice, and after a grudging few weeks of rest he returned to the forge. Although he would scarcely admit it, poverty as well as pride drove him back; by now he had published six books, but they had brought him virtually no financial reward, and his wages were so low that saving had been impossible. At the age of thirty-seven he was considered too young for the Civil List pension that his friends had applied for, but he was also too old to find fresh employment easily. Before many weeks had passed, however, Williams was finally compelled to leave the railway shop, and in September, soon after the declaration of war, he turned to market-gardening for his livelihood.

The emotions with which Williams was stirred in the early months of the Great War were typical enough of public feeling at that time, but they add nothing now to his poetic stature. His patriotism was well-intentioned, but his verses on such unedifying subjects as the *Rout of the Baby-killers* are distasteful and unworthy of their author. To those who have endured two world conflicts it is not easy to credit the debonair jingoism with which men of undoubted sensibility viewed the outbreak of hostilities in 1914. Williams later confessed that he had no great opinion of his verses at this time, but he had them published none the less and they sold rather better than his previous collections.

He badly needed the small amounts of money that his writings sometimes earned him. Market-gardening was a less stable source of income than the railway factory and the work was almost as hard; but he was able at times to bicycle around the district collecting material for a third book of Wiltshire memorials and an anthology of folk-songs. Neither of these undertakings was published until after the war, and work on them was interrupted in the winter of 1916 when he was called up, and passed as fit for home garrison duties.

The army brought certain financial advantages, and Williams found amongst the officers and his fellow-gunners an interest and sympathy that he had never experienced at Swindon. The soldiering life with its frequent moves from place to place intrigued him, and stimulated him to write commentaries on each fresh occurrence. He recorded everything, but indiscriminately and without distinction. Poetry, which required time for thought and meditation, was almost forgotten.

If Williams had been kept, as he should have been, on garrison duties at home his army career would have been an unexceptional interlude; instead, in September 1917, he was sent by ship to India. He was not an eager traveller, but he accepted this strange and unexpected adventure without complaint. There was a long and uncomfortable voyage by troopship round Africa to Bombay, and on arrival Williams's battery was posted to Roorkee in the United Provinces.

At first he judged all sights and scenery by the exacting standards of South Marston, and often they proved disappointing. "I like the birds best that more nearly resemble our own at home," he told Mary. Some weeks later, at Cawnpore, "as the wind blew, it reminded me of the hot blast and flame that used to come from the oil furnaces in the stamping shop," and he pined for "a white mist of rain sweeping over Liddington Hill down upon the valley." Gradually, however, the splendour and richness of India captured his imagination, and, like so many travellers to that land, once the immediate impressions of dirt and dust and squalor had been absorbed he fell under the spell of a country where nature, poetry, and religion were woven like interlocking strands in the fabric of everyday life.

The inevitable onslaught of minor tropical diseases and the fierce heat at Cawnpore did not deter him. He sought out information about all aspects of Indian life, attended religious services, visited places of interest, and wrote down everything that he had seen. But garrison towns in the plains did not really satisfy Williams's purposeful enthusiasm, and it was not until he was posted to Ranikhet that he experienced unalloyed happiness away from home.

Ranikhet is a hill station, 6,000 feet high, in the foothills of the Himalayas under the shadow of Nanda Devi. To the north an unbroken chain of mountains fills the sky, white and unchallengeable; all around are forests of pine and rhododendron rich with the flowers of the season, jasmine, roses, and delphinium. Williams was enchanted by everything he saw, but the great snow-peaks were to him the most wonderful and awful of all. Their remote beauty haunted him; "to look upon them is like a glimpse of eternity," he declared, and whenever he saw them his feelings were swayed between humbleness and exaltation.

The weeks he spent at Ranikhet were the high glory of his life. He scarcely took a walk without finding some new, or unexpectedly familiar flower or bird that he could write about to Mary. "Oh it's a jolly, jolly spot, and I just love it. The Himalayas are divine. It is great to see. What material I shall have for books—if I live. . . . I would not have missed India for five years of life."

The beauty of Ranikhet revived within him the creative inspiration that he had all but lost. For a time he gave up his attempts to write prose records of humdrum experiences in which he could interest no publisher. It was to poetry that he turned again to express his feelings, and for the last time in his life he wrote poem after poem, quickly and joyously, out of love for the place.

The verses that Williams wrote at this time were for the most part in a descriptive and meditative strain at which he excelled. Ranikhet offered an inexhaustible source of inspiration for a lover of nature and the high hills:

> Where Dawn puts forth her flame-white hand,
> And suns and moons successive rise,
> Lo! Trisul, Nandadevi stand
> And prop the empire of the skies.

Just as Liddington Hill was a beacon of locality to his Wiltshire poems, so at Ranikhet the serene, remote presence of the Himalayas formed an inescapable background to every mood and moment.

> The moon in her dream-like bliss steals forth
> And silvers the snows of the vacant north;
> A myriad fire-flies flicker and shine,
> And the glow-worm kindles her taper fine,
> Twinkling in the glooms
> Of ferns, and leaves, and blooms,
> And the soul of the night is poured like wine.

At times Ranikhet seemed to him an earthly paradise, and only Mary drew his thoughts back to England. He knew himself to be "a lonely sort of fellow," and through contemplation of the Himalayas he discovered a sympathetic loneliness, profounder and more detached than his own, amongst their aloof and inaccessible summits.

> For I am one with you, and ye are mine,
> And my immortal spirit penetrates
> Beyond the unimaginable spheres.

Williams had spent a good deal of his time in India studying the various religions, and the pantheistic elements of Hinduism echoed, in many respects, his own beliefs. The complete association of man with his natural environment, linked by a vital essence that impelled all things, rational and irrational, animate and inanimate, seemed only a logical step from the philosophy Jefferies had taught him. Williams had never seriously questioned the broad principles of the Christian ethic, but he was convinced that Hinduism, too, taught good morality, especially in providing a comforting faith to those who were rich only in the spirit. God, who watched over the restless fluctuations that built the changeless pattern of cosmic unity, gave to His worshippers an image of the Divine in all things and a freedom from the tyranny of their daily lives.

Williams took every opportunity that offered itself to learn and to discuss with Indians the tenets of their faith; and as was usual with him he used much of his newly gained knowledge in his poetry. In his enthusiasm he wrote to his friend Dowsing, "India . . . has imbued me with a different spirit. Its peculiar atmosphere suits me. Here is indeed poetry. Every tenth man you meet is a poet, and a darned great one, too. He writes nothing. But he is a poet. For poetry here is religion and religion is all poetry."

In England, Williams knew, poetry was far removed from daily life. Dowsing, who was making guns at the Vickers factory, could scarcely name one man in all Sheffield with whom he could share his love of verse: in India Williams found one in ten. Perhaps he was romanticizing, but it is possible that Williams saw an unspoilt, untempted agrarian community, surrounded by natural beauty and strong in religious belief, and that in his eyes it was Arcadian.

The search for Arcady is almost instinctive amongst poets. In England the setting is usually temperately pastoral, and seldom ventures on a landscape more unfamiliar than Sicily; but wherever Arcady has been conceived it has been thronged with lowly poets. In the plains of India Williams had become accustomed to a culture and customs utterly unfamiliar to his limited experience. In the hills the strangeness was transfigured and, undeceived by a knowledge of the language spoken around him, he may for a time have lived in such an Arcady.

Although he was not able to publish any books while he was in India, Williams found several outlets for his poems in the English-language newspapers. Of the collection that he brought with him when he reluctantly left Ranikhet in August 1918 one poem in particular deserves mention. It was, in effect, a survey of all that he had seen and found memorable during his nine months in India. Because it attempted to be definitive and precisely factual it is better as a letter home than as a studied display of Miltonic cadences. *India: A Poem* is a documentary of uneven quality. Williams was never sufficiently self-critical to realize when he was over-writing, and often by striving too hard he wastes the cumulative effect of whole passages by a phrase of bathos or a querulous judgment.

> the jaded city feels the heat
> Insufferable, in street or alley packed,
> Or stifling tenement, or dense bazaar,
> Reeking with noxious odours, while within
> His filthy den and sty contagious,
> Where foul disease and sickness propagate—
> Choleras, and fevers, and consumptions dire—
> Crouches the native, his dear *hooka* nursing,
> Expectorating freely in the sewer
> That flows before his door.

Innumerable incidents in the daily life of an Indian town are recorded in Williams's poem; nor does he forget to cast a professional eye over the state of agriculture in country districts. The general effect of the poem is necessarily of superficial impressions, but when his writing is most restrained he recreates incidents with freshness and charm; and the blank verse that ineffectually aped *Paradise Lost* in the passage above may (as in the fragment that follows) be more happily compared to the narrated stories of *The Prelude*.

> The poor snake-charmer comes, a dreamy youth,
> With figure slender, soft and delicate,
> Ill-matched with trade so dire and dangerous.
> He, loosing from their secret dark abode
> His slimy serpents, and the hooded cobra
> With gleaming eyes, erect, and sibilant,
> Tames them to gentleness with notes low-breathed
> From his weird instrument, and departs well-pleased
> With the small offerings profusely made.

No description of India that Williams wrote could dwell for long on the plains, and in the second part of his poem we follow the course of his journey up into the hills at Ranikhet. The enthusiasm with which he greets the Himalayas is so obvious that he scarcely needs to assure his readers that he was "contented with the fate that brought me hither." For the rest of the poem he extols the beauties of his beloved Ranikhet.

> pleasant it is,
> When the high sun looks outward to the west
> And streams above the snowy mountain-tops,
> To feel the cool wind wafting through the leaves
> Laden with scents of flowers well-beloved—
> Primrose and violet, lily, rose, and pink,
> Jasmine, and hyacinth, and columbine,
> And fragrant orchis, sitting there at ease
> Musing amid the new-found paradise.

Williams returned to the plains expecting to be demobilized and sent home. But there were delays, and he fretted away the weeks in the heat, longing to get back to South Marston. There was bad news from home: his house was to be sold, and he had no prospect of getting another. His health was not improving, and apart from the plot of land on which he could continue to grow fruit and vegetables he was faced at the age of forty-two with the prospect of unemployment and renewed poverty. Only Mary remained constant and uncomplaining, and it was to her that he returned in the autumn of 1919, with no more resources than the manuscripts of three unpublished books and an indomitable will to work.

The story of the next ten years makes melancholy reading. The resilience of Williams's youth could not be revived in middle age. Disasters weighed increasingly heavily, and the immediate future became a more desperate consideration than of old. The hundred and one small troubles that beset and harry the really poor began gradually to deaden his creative energies. When first he returned to Wiltshire he found he had a little local fame. He was able to earn some money here and there with lectures and magazine articles, but for the books he had written when he was in the army he could find no publisher. He was not entirely surprised, as he realized that they lacked the inspiration of his earlier compositions. "I *felt* more strongly when I was at the factory," he told Dowsing, "and wrote my best things then. The work was obnoxious, but the daily release gave me opportunity. It was the contrast and I always *felt intensely* at the weekend. And you have the wherewithal to live and keep your family. Now I have practically nothing."

His friends obtained a grant for him from the Royal Literary Fund. It was only £20, but it tided him over until his garden began to yield some return for the labour that Mary and he expended upon it. He found himself unable to work so hard as before, and a succession of illnesses interrupted him.

As a climax to his troubles he was forced to leave his house. With typical determination he set about building a new one for himself, on his own land and aided only by his wife. They used the stones from a tumbledown cottage in the village and carted bricks from the derelict locks of a nearby canal. Throughout the winter of 1920–21 the two of them worked without remission, exhausted by the heavy labour, but convinced that with a home of their own they could live off the land. Their house was plain and sturdy; one would scarcely notice it today except by the plaque that has now been added above the porch, but for Alfred and Mary Williams it was much more than a four-square stone cottage trimmed with brick; it was a proud monument to hard work and an act of faith in the future. They called it "Ranikhet."

Soon after "Ranikhet" was built Williams was able to put the finishing touches to two books that had remained uncompleted all the time he had been in the army. Duckworth published both of them, *Round about the Upper Thames* in 1922, and *Folk-songs of the Upper Thames* the following year. The folk-songs make an interesting volume, and Williams's efforts to collect them together were timely as the singers and their songs were fast dying out in Wiltshire. The book contains some six hundred examples of ballad and song that Williams patiently and tactfully coaxed old people to repeat to him. In such an anthology, one might naturally assume, resides the truly peasant poetry of Wiltshire. But folk-song, Williams stresses in his preface, seldom originates from the country. All but a dozen of the songs he records were composed in London or some large town, and although the spirit of the old poetry that Williams so dearly loved seems to epitomize rural England, it is only because time and change move more leisurely in country districts that the ballad-mongers' ditties survived in Wiltshire long after they had been forgotten in the places of their birth.

Another interesting feature of Williams's anthology is the almost complete absence of dialect writing. One would have expected even town-bred rhymes to acquire the accent of their adopted home in course of time, and Edward Slow's verses show what a pungent and distinct speech-form Wiltshire produced. But dialect writing, Williams declared, was a comparatively recent introduction, and sprang not from the peasantry but from educated men with an experimental interest in phonetics. "The villagers speak dialect, but do not care to read it. They are shocked and offended when they see their own language written. The townspeople do not speak dialect, but like to read it." Barnes's poetry, and probably Relph's, bear out Williams's supposition; certainly it is possible that the increased volume of dialect writing during the past century bears some relationship to the minute, academic interest that has also been lavished on antiquarianism.

The publication of the folk-songs gave Williams great pleasure. In addition to being an undertaking of no little magnitude, he regarded the book as a fitting culmination to his other Wiltshire studies. He felt that he had left behind him a complete record of a rural community at a time when old memories and customs were dying, and a new pattern of life was taking their place.

Williams did not understand the changes that were transforming even rural Wiltshire in the years after the war. Partly to escape from the alien encroachments of the twentieth century, and partly because he was never happy without some formidable project to wrestle with, he started to teach himself Sanskrit. When he was in India the philosophy of the Vedas had attracted him. Now he needed some such consolation to lift him above the miseries of his daily life. He convinced himself of the importance of reading the sacred books of Hinduism in their original tongue, and set to work with all the enthusiasm at his command. "I suppose I may be a little *abnormal* in my love for it," he commented; but it was not in him to be half-hearted about any scheme that he undertook.

No amount of Sanskrit could earn him a living, and despite his dreams of self-sufficiency when "Ranikhet" was built he found that his market-garden was a precarious source of income. Peas failed, and the birds devoured his strawberries. He could no longer regard such calamities with equanimity. The poet who had written *To a Blackbird* twelve years before, "Earth would be poorer for the loss of thee," now swore to exterminate every one he saw. It was a joyless, dour struggle that he was engaged in, and the enemy was nature who would not yield him sustenance.

Now and then the ill-fortune that pursued him seemed to relent a little. The Royal Literary Fund authorized a further grant, and at the end of 1923 a payment of £150 was made to him from the Royal Bounty Fund in recognition of his literary work. But however carefully he husbanded such gifts they were soon expended, and they brought no security with them for the future. Once again Williams's application for a Civil List pension was turned down on account of his comparative youth. He tried desperately to write books and get them published. Old manuscripts were revised and new projects embarked upon, but always without success.

Galloway Kyle, who had long held the material, did issue Williams's *Selected Poems* in 1925. Apart from the Indian poems, which had never been printed in book form, most of these verses had been included in the volumes published by Erskine Macdonald before the war. *Selected Poems* is a handsome book, despite numerous misprints that irked Williams, and a fine memorial to a poetic career; for by the time it was published the author could spare little time for verse. Sanskrit occupied every leisure moment, and he was already engaged on his last great project, a translation of the *Panchatantra*.

The constant alternation of hard physical and mental work gave him less exhilaration than of old. As the 'twenties drew to a close he became more of a recluse, hating to admit even the unspoken sympathy of his friends. By day he worked dourly on his unprofitable patch of ground: in the evenings he tussled, with a certain intellectual pride, to translate his *Tales from the Panchatantra*, for which there was no hope of profit, and little prospect of a publisher.

There seemed no obvious end to the hand-to-mouth existence that Alfred and Mary Williams had been leading for so many years. The creative instinct and the zest for life had withered: only intellect and a stubborn will remained. They had the comfort and company of one another, and life, though hard, was bearable when they were together.

The climax was sudden, and tragic in its coming. Early in 1930, after a winter of small illnesses, it was discovered that Mary was suffering from an incurable disease. She was taken to hospital in Swindon and an operation was attempted. It failed, and Williams was told that she had only a few weeks to live. No comfort was possible, and Williams's grief was agonizing. "My dear wife is more than my right hand: she was a great part of my very life," he wrote to one friend, and to another he asked in his despair, "Why do we love each other so?"

The spirit of endurance that had supported him through so many hardships was, he suddenly realized, only partly his own. Mary had been so close a partner that the thought of her death sapped even his will to live. Throughout the dark months of February and March Williams bicycled every day to Swindon to visit Mary. During the hours when he was left to himself he took long walks through the wintry countryside, or roamed restlessly around the house that he had taken such pride in building. But he was pursued by misery, finding some dear association in every object and every thought.

There were two crumbs of comfort that would have cheered him at any other time, but now they passed almost unnoticed. Basil Blackwell accepted *Tales from the Panchatantra* for publication, and Ramsay MacDonald, the third Prime Minister to be petitioned, granted Williams the Civil List pension that would have freed him from some of his financial worries.

But Williams was inconsolable. The whole focus of his world narrowed around the bedside of his dying wife. The nervous strain of the prolonged and painful parting became intolerable, and his friends were helpless to relieve him of his burden of grief. On April 9th he visited the hospital for the last time, and returned to "Ranikhet" in agony of mind and body. In the night his heart failed him, and he died.

A Word for Today

Southey was rash to predict that in his day the uneducated poet no longer existed, and it would be almost as foolhardy to do so today. The purely peasant-poet may never be heard again in our land, for the peasantry is scarcely recognizable as a distinct group in our present society; but the artisan and the labourer will still find from time to time, within their own ranks, men like Williams with a natural gift for poetry.

The struggle to be heard will never be so poignant, though to exist by the writing of verse is as difficult now as it has ever been. No longer shall we hear of pathetic attempts to achieve literacy before a poetic soul can be unburdened. Universal education and the widespread dissemination of the printed word have broken down some of the barriers that hindered genius in the past. The complexity of the world today in which both countrymen and townsmen in some measure participate does not exclude the poet of natural simplicity. To write from the heart requires no training, and although it is a gift that few are born with and fewer still acquire, there cannot be many parishes in England even now that do not house a writer of verses, though none of real merit has achieved the dignity of print in recent years.

The poets are not lacking, nor will the subjects of poetry ever be exhausted. Greater dangers in this present age are the almost total extinction of personal patronage and the enormous quantity of books that are published every year. In a haphazard way the State has taken to itself some of the functions of the private patron, but inevitably it is a poor substitute. Spence, Southey, and Capel Lofft could cast a watchful eye over the entire field of literary production in their day. They were able to help and encourage writers at the very beginning of their careers. No single man would be able to do so now. Lordly patrons, whose names are familiar today only from the dedications they inspired, were prepared to gamble on, and able to support, struggling authors in a manner that would be financially impossible for anyone in our present, heavily-taxed society. Even the most sympathetic form of State patronage would be unable to run the risks that a private individual might take in supporting an unfledged poet at the very time when help is most needed.

The present lack of responsibility on the part of the reading public for its indigent authors is not only a financial problem. A guild system in literature, as in other crafts, may outgrow its own strength. The last century has stimulated such an impressive increase both in the writing and reading of books by all sections of the community that the actions of any individual are relatively of slight importance. The field has become so open that although a poet may easily appear in print without the aid of a patron, he will never command any undivided attention. The quieter his voice and message the more difficult it will be to obtain a hearing. A peasant or artisan poet of today will no longer be looked on as a curiosity or a freak, but will be judged solely by the healthier critical standards of his excellence as a poet. But an innate feeling of inferiority might well deter some poorly-educated young poets from attempting direct competition with their intellectually better-equipped contemporaries; particularly as the current fashions of poetry favour a more subjective method of expression than a peasant-poet is usually able to grasp.

Outward disadvantages will never discourage a determined poet. Burns or Clare would have written poetry whether they achieved recognition in their own day or not; but Duck or Bloomfield might well have ceased to compose verses as they grew older, and disregarded the effusions of their youth if they had been cold-shouldered by the world of letters. The loss to literature may seem insignificant, but our poetic heritage, rich as it is, would be the poorer if a single voice was discouraged into silence.

Select Bibliography

WORKS OF GENERAL REFERENCE

Beattie, James, *The Minstrel: or the Progress of Genius* (Book I, London, 1771. Book II, London, 1774).

Blunden, Edmund, *Nature in English Literature* (London, 1929).

Burns, Robert, *The Complete Works* (London and Glasgow, 1937).

Fitz-Herbert, Sir Anthony, *The Boke of Husbandry*, ed. W. W. Skeat (Reprinted from the edition of 1534, London, 1882).

Fordham, Montague, *A Short History of English Rural Life from the Anglo-Saxon Invasion to the Present Time* (London, 1916).

Fordham, Montague and T. R., *The English Agricultural Labourer 1300–1925* (London, 1925).

Garnier, Russell Montague, *Annals of the British Peasantry* (London, 1895).

Hammond, John Laurence LeBreton and Lucy Barbara, *The Village Labourer 1760–1832* (4th ed., London, 1927).

Hazlitt, William, *Lectures on English Poets* and *The Spirit of the Age* (Everyman's Library, London, 1910).

Heath-Stubbs, John, *The Darkling Plain* (London, 1950).

Howitt, William, *The Rural Life of England* (2 vols., London, 1838).

Jones, John, *Attempts in Verse by John Jones, an Old Servant with Some Account of the Writer, Written by Himself and an Introductory Essay on the Lives and Works of our Uneducated Poets by Robert Southey, Esq., Poet Laureate* (London, 1831).

Mandeville, Bernard De, *The Fable of the Bees: or, Private Vices Publick Benefits* (2nd ed., with additions including "An Essay on Charity and Charity-Schools," London, 1723).

Moritz, Carl Philipp, *Travels in England in 1782* (Reprinted from the Edition of 1795, London, 1924).

Reynolds, Myra, *The Treatment of Nature in English Poetry between Pope and Wordsworth* (2nd ed., Chicago, 1909).

Seebohm, Mabel Elizabeth (M. E. Christie), *The Evolution of the English Farm* (London, 1927).

Shairp, John Campbell, *On Poetic Interpretation of Nature* (Edinburgh, 1877).

Tinker, Chauncey Brewster, *Nature's Simple Plan: A Phase of Radical Thought in the mid-Eighteenth Century* (Princeton and London, 1922).

Trevelyan, George Macaulay, *English Social History* (London, 1944).

Waring, Elijah, *Recollections and Anecdotes of E. Williams* (Iolo Morganwg), (London, 1850).

Wordsworth, William, *Literary Criticism*, ed. C. Nowell Smith (London, 1905).

WILLIAM BARNES

Orra: A Lapland Tale (Dorchester, 1822).

Poems of Rural Life, in the Dorset Dialect (With a Dissertation on the Folk Speech, and a Glossary of Dorset Words, Dorchester and London, 1844).

Poems, partly of Rural Life (In National English, London, 1846).

A Philological Grammar (Grounded upon English, and formed from a comparison of more than sixty languages. Being an introduction to the science of grammar, and a help to grammars of all languages, especially English, Latin, and Greek, London, 1854).

Hwomely Rhymes (A second collection of Dorset Poems, London, 1859).

"Thoughts on Beauty and Art," *Macmillan's Magazine*, IV (1861), pp. 126–37.

Tiw: or, a View on the roots and stems of the English as a Teutonic tongue (London, 1862).

Third Collection of Poems in the Dorset Dialect (London, 1862).

A Grammar and Glossary of the Dorset Dialect (With the History, Outspreading, and Bearings of South-Western English, Transactions of the Philological Society, Berlin, 1863).

Poems of Rural Life in Common English (London, 1868).

An Outline of English Speech-Craft (London, 1878).

An Outline of Rede-Craft, or Logic (With English Wording, London, 1880).

A Glossary of the Dorset Dialect (With a Grammar of its Word Shapening and Wording, Dorchester and London, 1886).

Leader Scott (Lucy Baxter), *The Life of William Barnes, Poet and Philologist* (London and New York, 1887).

Hardy, Thomas, ed., *Select Poems of William Barnes* (London, 1908).

Grigson, Geoffrey, *The Harp of Aeolus and other essays on Art, Literature and Nature* (London, 1948), pp. 98–122.

Grigson, Geoffrey, ed., *Selected Poems of William Barnes* (London, 1950).

Dugdale, Arthur G., *William Barnes of Dorset* (London, 1953).

ROBERT BLOOMFIELD

The Farmer's Boy: A Rural Poem (London, 1800).

The Poems of Robert Bloomfield (3 vols., London, 1827).

Hart, William H., ed., *Selections from the Correspondence of Robert Bloomfield* (London, 1870).

Gant, Roland, ed., *A Selection of Poems by Robert Bloomfield* (London, 1947).

A collection of unpublished letters in the British Museum.

JOHN FREDERICK BRYANT

Verses by J. F. Bryant . . . together with his life, written by himself (London, 1787).

JOHN CLARE

Poems Descriptive of Rural Life and Scenery (London, 1820).

The Village Minstrel, and Other Poems (2 vols., London, 1821).

The Shepherd's Calendar, with Village Stories and Other Poems (London, 1827).

The Rural Muse (London, 1835).

Gale, Norman, ed., *Poems by John Clare* (Rugby, 1901).

Symons, Arthur, ed., *Poems by John Clare* (London, 1908).

Blunden, Edmund, and Porter, Alan, eds., *Poems, chiefly from Manuscript* (London, 1920).

Blunden, Edmund, ed., *Madrigals and Chronicles* (London, 1924).

Blunden, Edmund, ed., *Sketches in the Life of John Clare, Written by Himself* (London, 1931).

Tibble, John William, and Anne, *John Clare: A Life* (London, 1932).

Tibble, John William, ed., *The Poems of John Clare* (2 vols., London, 1935).

Grigson, Geoffrey, ed., *Poems of John Clare's Madness* (London, 1949).

Grigson, Geoffrey, ed., *Selected Poems* (London, 1950).

Tibble, John William and Anne, eds., *The Prose of John Clare* (London, 1951).

Tibble, John William, and Anne, eds., *The Letters of John Clare* (London, 1951).

Wilson, June, *Green Shadows: the Life of John Clare* (London, 1951).

MARY COLLIER

The Woman's Labour: An Epistle to Mr. Stephen Duck, in Answer to his Late Poem, called The Thresher's Labour (London, 1739).

Poems on Several Occasions (With some remarks on Her Life, Winchester, 1762).

GEORGE CRABBE

The Village: a poem in two books (London, 1783).

The Borough: a poem, in twenty-four letters (London, 1810).

Carlyle, Alexander J. and Rebecca M., eds., *The Poetical Works*, (London, 1908).

Blunden, Edmund, ed., *The Life of George Crabbe, by his Son*, (London, 1947).

ROBERT DODSLEY

A Muse in Livery: or, The Footman's Miscellany (London, 1732).

STEPHEN DUCK

Poems on Several Subjects (A pirated volume, London, 1730).

Poems on Several Occasions (With an account of the author by J. Spence, London, 1736).

Thomson, Katherine, ed., *Memoirs of Viscountess Sundon, Mistress of the Robes to Queen Caroline* (2 vols., London, 1847).

Davis, Rose M., *Stephen Duck, the Thresher Poet* (Orono, University of Maine Studies, II, 8, 1926).

WILLIAM FALCONER

The Shipwreck: a poem in three cantos (London, 1762).

JOSIAH RELPH

A Miscellany of Poems (Glasgow, 1747).

ROBERT TATERSAL

The Bricklayer's Miscellany: Containing Poems on Several Subjects (Part I, 2nd ed., London, 1734. Part II, London, 1735).

JOHN TAYLOR

Works . . . Comprised in the folio edition of 1630 (3 vols., Manchester: The Spenser Society, 1869).

Works . . . Not included in the folio edition of 1630 (5 vols., Manchester: The Spenser Society, 1870–78).

JAMES THOMSON

Winter, a poem (London, 1726).

Summer: a poem (London, 1727).

Spring: a poem (London, 1728).

The Seasons (London, 1730).

Robertson, James Logie, ed., The Complete Poetical Works (Oxford, 1908).

Macaulay, George Campbell, James Thomson (English Men of Letters, London, 1908).

THOMAS TUSSER

A hundreth good pointes of husbandrie (London, 1557).

Five hundred pointes of good Husbandrie, as well for the Champion, or open countrie, as also for the woodland, or seuerall etc. (London, 1580).

Mavor, William, ed., Five Hundred points of Good Husbandry (London, 1812).

HENRY KIRKE WHITE

Clifton Grove, a sketch in verse, with other poems (London, 1803).

The Remains of Henry Kirke White (With an account of his life by Robert Southey, 3 vols., London, 1808–22).

The Poetical and Prose Works (With a life by Robert Southey, London, 1864).

ALFRED WILLIAMS

Songs in Wiltshire (London, 1909).

Poems in Wiltshire (London, 1911).

A Wiltshire Village (London, 1912).

Nature and Other Poems (London, 1912).

Cor Cordium (London, 1913).

Villages of the White Horse (London, 1913).

Life in a Railway Factory (London, 1915).

War Sonnets and Songs (London, 1916).

Round about the Upper Thames (London, 1922).

(Ed.) *Folk-songs of the Upper Thames* (With an Essay on Folk-song activity in the Upper Thames neighbourhood, London, 1923).

Selected Poems (London, 1926).

Clark, Leonard, *Alfred Williams, His Life and Work* (Bristol, 1945).

JAMES WOODHOUSE

Woodhouse, Reginald I., ed., *The Life and Poetical Works* (2 vols., London, 1896).

ANN YEARSLEY

Poems on Several Occasions (With a Prefatory Letter by Hannah More, London, 1785).

Poems on Various Subjects (With Hannah More's prefatory letter to the author's previous work, and "Mrs. Y's Narrative" exculpating herself from the charge of ingratitude to Hannah More, London, 1787).

INDEX

GEORGE ALLEN & UNWIN LTD
London: 40 Museum Street, W.C.1

Auckland: Haddon Hall, City Road
Sydney, N.S.W.: Bradbury House, 55 York Street
Cape Town: 58–60 Long Street
Bombay: 15 Graham Road, Ballard Estate, Bombay 1
Calcutta: 17 Chittaranjan Avenue, Calcutta 13
New Delhi: Munshi Niketan, Kamla Market, Ajmeri Gate, New Delhi 1
Karachi: Haroon Chambers, South Napier Road, Karachi 2
Toronto: 91 Wellington Street West
Sao Paulo: Avenida 9 de Julho 1138–Ap. 51

THE EVOLUTION OF THE ENGLISH FARM

M. E. SEEBOHM

Demy 8vo   Revised Second Edition   30s. net

'This is a work of the first importance to all students of social and economic history. It is a veritable encyclopaedia of information . . . The value is enormously increased by the eminently readable style in which the authoress has so admirably succeeded in expressing herself.' *Antiquity*

'It is written with great care in a clear and interesting style, and no one who takes any interest in . . . country life can afford to miss it.' *Sunday Times*

HOW TO WRITE A PARISH HISTORY

R. B. PUGH

L. Cr. 8vo   8s. 6d. net

Much local history is written by amateurs about their own neighbourhoods, but whilst there are great advantages in this course, the standard reached is not invariably so high as the writers would themselves wish. This is due as much as anything to a lack of guidance. *How to Write a Parish History* has been written to help those engaged in the attractive pastime of local history to use their sources wisely and to arrange their material logically. In the main, Mr. Pugh's book is arranged topically, separate sections being devoted to such subjects as the manor, the parish, communications and population. Each section points out the essential features to look for, and directs the inquirer to the most reliable sources and works of reference.

THE GULF OF THE YEARS

LETTERS FROM JOHN RUSKIN TO KATHLEEN OLANDER

Edited with an Introduction by RAYNER UNWIN

L. Cr. 8vo   9s. 6d. net

'The book which every library must possess if it seeks to provide a complete picture of Ruskin. More than that, it is a delight to read, in spite of the sorrow of the theme, for the reflection it gives of a lovable and admirable girl, and for the illumination of a great writer in his last days of hope.' EVELYN WAUGH in the *Spectator*.

LONDON: GEORGE ALLEN & UNWIN LTD.